When Six Audacious Leaders Had The Gall To Succeed

Bavani Periasamy . Freda Liu . Fu-En Yee
Norlida Azmi . Sharma Kumari . Syireen Rose

HOW DARE THEY

When Six Audacious Leaders Had The Gall To Succeed
978-629-97147-2-9 (Print)
978-629-7626-07-9 (eBook)

Published by Inspiration Hub
(under I Hub Concept Sdn Bhd)
Email: *team@theinspirationhub.com*

Editor: Ahmad Azrai
Cover Designer: Justin Wong
Author Portraits Illustrator: Wan Nadra Imany binti Wan Adli Ridzwan

Table of Contents

Chapter 3: Being Audacious Pays........................133

Chapter 4: Beyond Audacity 203

Acknowledgements

To my co-authors Freda, Sharma, Syireen, Bavani, and Oli (Norlida): Thank you so much for saying "YES!" right at the very beginning when I brought up this project. Without all of you, this book wouldn't have turned up the way it is now. It took quite an effort to keep to the deadlines and commitment to strive together for this good purpose. From the bottom of my heart, all of you are my phenomenal audacious sisters! All of you played your part so well. Despite the personal busy schedules and hectic work demands, we have all made it this far. Thank you!

To my family members, great buddies, and supportive fans: Thank you for always being my strongest pillars in all that I do. Love you all to the moon and back!

To Nickey Teoh of Inspiration Hub: Thank you for trusting our work and making this book a reality. Your support in our work makes it so easy for us to say: "Yes, we want Nickey to publish our book!" My utmost appreciation for every effort you put in to meet many demands of our audacious sisters!

To our editor Ahmad Azrai: Thank you for stringing our individual pieces into such a beautiful flow. It takes great energy to work around the clock to meet our tight deadline, dancing backwards and forwards to meet our beats. We value your contribution to our project!

I'm indeed so blessed to receive all the "Yeses", and may these "Yeses" from everyone – near and far, seen and unseen – continue to shower miracles on you as you work on your Audacity to become your audacious self, to realise your audacious dream(s), and to live up to your audacious life!

Fu-En Yee

Foreword

When I first started out as a professional speaker and then as an author, many colleagues thought I was audacious to even think about doing these things. As a young high school student, I had read Jonathan Swift's *Gulliver's Travels* where he had described his travels to the world of tiny humans and giants. I enjoyed reading it because of the book's narrative.

Swift said: "May you live every day of your life." A life without purpose and passion is wasted. The goal is to live every day of your life while you are alive. The aim is to do and accomplish something, to help others achieve their dreams, and to be kind. In my journey as a professional speaker and author, the greatest satisfaction that I have derived is in sharing my experiences with people, and hoping that my audience will benefit from them.

Six high-achieving women – fellow members of the Malaysian Association of Professional Speakers (MAPS) – have embarked upon an audacious journey to write this book, *How Dare They*. Each one of them is an accomplished high-achiever, and each is an outstanding professional. Fu-En Yee, the initiator of this book, is a client-centred psychotherapist with a vision to create a better world. Syireen Rose is a wordsmith who has excelled in the communication field; meanwhile, Freda Liu is one of Malaysia's outstanding media personalities. Norlida Azmi is a passionate advocate of well-being; Sharma is a passionate learning and development professional with a mission to help people learn; and Bavani strongly calls for all of us to be truly grateful in our lives.

The drive to share and make this world a better place is evident in their writings. When I was writing one of my books, I was startled to read *The Audacity of Hope* by former US President Barack Obama. Obama's message of hope was not rooted in wilful ignorance nor blind optimism, but in something more substantial. He talked about people dreaming about doing impossible things, whether it was about slaves singing freedom songs, or about immigrants in small boats trying to reach the shores. Talking about himself, Obama said it was a skinny kid with a funny name and a different colour of skin who aspired to become the President of the United States of America, and who believed the nation had a place for him despite all the challenges. It was hope in the face of difficulty; hope in the face of uncertainty – THAT was the audacity of hope.

How Dare They is a collective guide from six authentic women who describe the need for both men and women to be authentic, and to take courageous action to create the outcomes that they truly want and hope to achieve. In a simple yet powerful way, they share and describe their experiences alongside related case studies, and what they learnt from them.

Audacity is about being brave and hopeful; you will find *How Dare They* a game changer if you truly wish to step out of the shadows and be an inspiration for others.

Tan Sri Dato' Dr. R. Palan
Pro Chancellor
University of Cyberjaya

Raison d'Être

The Reason

Perhaps the story of empowerment and women warriors is getting stale – and yet the concerns of gender equality prevails. Perhaps it is about more than just men and women being equal, and more about understanding what it takes to be a man and to be a woman. Perhaps it is human nature to succumb to drama and whine because nothing seems to be working the way that it should be. Perhaps, it is just "perhaps" – and everything is just in our minds.

This book, however, is a firm stand that everybody – regardless of whether you are men or women, child or adult, infant or elderly – experiences similar struggles in life to achieve the wisdom that they deservingly need to a complete BEING. We learn about love and hate; we learn about joy and pain; we learn about hope and disappointment; we learn about gain and loss; we learn about good and evil – and just like that, we have ALL learned the same values in life.

If we experience the same emotions and are exposed to the same values, how are we different, then? That's where this book – written by six powerful individuals who have experienced life, and who like everybody else have tasted the bitter and the sweet – can help.

As authors of this book, it is our stance that **the outcome lies solely in the actions taken**.

The twist to these stories lies in the pathways we undertook to face life – and how audaciously we decided to live it. We wrote because we believe that **we are all – at the core – the same**: looking for peace, harmony, love and abundance.

We believe that everybody has been audacious at least once in our lifetime – so why not every time?

Biographies

 **Fu-En Yee** is a heart-centric international Psychotherapist with a vision to create a better future for Humanity. Missionary and unconditional, she dedicates her time to help people to align their head to their heart and break-free from unsupportive subconscious beliefs, in order to create a purposeful and meaningful life. While busy changing the lives of clients from 13 countries across four continents, Fu-En is also an international Speaker, Coach, and Author, with her debut book being called *Boss, Your Wish Is Your Command!*. At the point of writing, she serves as the Vice President – International & Social Affairs for the Malaysian Association of Professional Speakers (MAPS). Fu-En has been named as one of the Most Successful People in Malaysia by Britishpedia Vol. III, and has been widely featured by both domestic and international media.

Bavani Periasamy has always been passionate about the area of learning and development from a young age as she comes from a family of educators. She is also very curious about understanding a person's cognitive abilities and behavioural characteristics. This has led Bavani to study and get certifications on psychometric assessment tools, and her experience in sales for more than 10 years has helped a lot in getting to know human behaviours. Her focus area of work now is on Gratitude and Happiness, for both individuals and for application of this at work to build a harmonious working environment.

Freda Liu is well-known as a radio broadcast journalist at BFM89.9. A powerhouse communicator and connector, she wears many hats as a global speaker for women empowerment and personal branding, an author of five books, an emcee, a highly sought-after moderator for corporate events, and a trainer. Freda has lived and breathed business in the past decade with Malaysia's leading business radio station, having conducted more than 5,000 interviews with prominent international names. An advocate for improvement in sustainability and women empowerment, she is an ambassador for the Women of Global Change KL Chapter, and a WASH (Clean Water & Sanitary Hygiene) advocate for World Vision Malaysia.

Norlida Azmi (Oli) is a passionate advocate for diversity, equity, and inclusion (DEI); digital; well-being; and sustainability. She is currently the Group Chief People Officer of Axiata and also serves as a NINED on edotco Group. Oli is an Adjunct Professor for Organisational Behaviour and Leadership at UNITAR International University's Graduate School. She spent more than 18 years overseas; Singapore, London, Riyadh, Doha, Dubai and Abu Dhabi. Oli has had a portfolio of diverse roles as Business Head, Risk Manager, COO, Strategic Planning Head, and CHRO with global and regional companies including Citibank, Standard Chartered, HSBC, ME banks, as well as UEM Group and PNB.

Sharma Kumari is the Founder-Consultant of Step by Stepz, and is a HR-Talent Management Strategist. She works with organisations to align talent and business strategy for sustainable business goals. Sharma's multi-industry experience includes leading cross-functional teams in key projects from foreign acquisitions to business ventures. With an MA in Communication Management, her background in behavioral communication and change management enriches her HR-Talent Management solutions. Sharma has managed a wide range of international assignments across more than 15 countries in Asia-Pacific, Europe, and North America. She is also a Faculty Member of the Human Capital Institute, USA, as well as an Associate Facilitator for Inspire Group Asia.

Syireen Rose is known as the WordSmith, and has more than two decades of experience in the Communication field, ranging from Public Relations to Branding; Copywriting to Ghostwriting; Authoring books; and now, for her passion with the Power of Words, she coaches communicators, leaders, and entrepreneurs on how to self-express with clarity and – most importantly – in integrity. Her most recent endeavours thrusted her into the world of networking and leadership, where she is coined as the TheWORD Coach and where she consults and coaches C-suites and business owners. Syireen is also the Executive Director of BNI Klang Valley South where she supports more than 250 business owners (and counting) to access business opportunities via a global network. She is the author of *Leadership is Ssshhh…* and a contributing author to *Why are you so Stupid!*. Syireen has several e-books, both published and unpublished, focused on communication and entrepreneurism. At the time of writing, she is the President of the Women Entrepreneur Network Association (WENA),

EXCO of the Malaysian Association for Professional
Speakers (MAPS), and Treasurer of KoperasiWENA
(KOWENA).

Introduction

Bavani Periasamy is a motivational speaker and business consultant who can be considered a Guru of Gratitude; then we have Freda Liu, a communicator extraordinaire who has covered the gamut of speaker, author, broadcast journalist, emcee, moderator, and trainer.

Fu-En Yee is a former corporate leader turned psychotherapist and first-time author (which was launched in 2022 itself – looks like the writing bug caught); meanwhile, Norlida Azmi – who is affectionately more famously known as Oli – is a professional people person, who holds the post of Group Chief People Officer for the Axiata Group AND Adjunct Professor for UNITAR.

Sharma Kumari is the Founder-Consultant of Step by Stepz, Malaysia, alongside her various roles as faculty member and coach for several institutions of higher education as well training houses; and finally, we have Syireen Rose, within whose slender frame beats the heart of an entrepreneur, a wordsmith, TheWORD Coach, and a BNI Executive Director – a ferocious flower indeed (just like the woody perennial plant that she is named after).

So what on Earth convinced these six disparate souls to come together and decide to write *How Dare They*, a book about "audacity"? And to write it in a such a way that the result is not a joint blend of all their voices but an actual showcase of each exclusive point of view stacked together side-by-side?

(Imagine, if you will, creating a gown whereby six different designers were called in and told to run free with their imaginations!)

How extraordinary! How unique!

How deliciously audacious.

So, of course, that justifies everything.

But what's even more astonishing is that despite the discreetly diverse backgrounds of these diverse doyens of business, they all have displayed shared traits that are uncanny:

- They have all had to suffer being misunderstood – to various degrees of harshness.

- They have all been in leadership roles that were thrust on to them when they were at such a tender age that they could not refuse.

- They have all seen success and failure enough times to not become bothered by such temporary and fleeting conditions.

- They share a healthy respect and devotion for an inspirational figure in their life, whether it is someone they personally know or whether it is someone to be admired.

- They are not doing what they are doing for the money or the fame – but they are doing it because they want to share their message and help as many people as possible along the way.

More importantly, they all seem to agree – without any outside prompting or intervention – on the most important part about being audacious: being true to one's self.

Seen from that point of view, it makes sense that we get six different narratives that do not gel – because even though the stories and experiences are distinctive, they have more than enough shared elements between them to enhance their sister narratives while still remaining true to their own individual voices. The topics are split into four parts:

- **Chapter 1: Audacity is a Big Word** deals with what the audacious word is all about;

- **Chapter 2: How to Be Audacious** talks about the ways this can be achieved;

- **Chapter 3: Being Audacious Pays** answers the question WHY you might want to be audacious; and

- **Chapter 4: Beyond Audacity** is all about what all of it will ultimately mean to you and to those around you.

It can definitely get a bit confusing at the start – but repeated readings should solve that problem. And each of the individual ladies are certainly more than happy to explain themselves in even greater detail (dear God), despite some of them being on a certain side of the introversion spectrum.

It's definitely worth repeated readings. In all those different takes, there is surely a take that is right for YOU; a message that hits all the right spots, and answers all of the questions in your head – lessons that you can learn to undertake your own journey into audacity, if you have yet to begin.

And what if you don't find anything that fits that bill? Well, then you will have discovered what **doesn't** work for you – and therefore, you can go in your own direction to find your own voice, your own truths, and your own conviction.

That would certainly qualify as audacity – the kind that we welcome here!

Tan Sri Dato' Sri Dr. Noorul Ainur Mohd. Nur
Chairman
University College of Yayasan Pahang

CHAPTER 1
Audacity is a Big Word

Embrace Your Inner Audacity

by Fu-En Yee

Audacious was a dirty word. When I came across this word during my interactions with mentors in my late 30s, it didn't occur to me to want to be associated with the word. Perhaps it was because "audacious" sounded too foreign to me then – or maybe I didn't hear it enough times in my daily communications to have it registered into my personal dictionary.

Or most likely, my subconscious mind rejected the word because I often heard people using it in reference to negativity.

Even when you google for "audacious meaning", most of the articles will explain it simply as "taking bold steps". While some would coin it rather negatively like "intrepidly daring", "recklessly bold", and "impudent lack of respect", there were others that painted "audacious" in a slightly more positive was, such as "marked by originality and verve", "unconventional", and "courageous".

These were not labels that I liked, although I had accustomed myself to the tag-words "brave" and "bold" ever since being introduced – at the very tender age of 7 – to the world of leadership by my grandfather. My labels were then expanded to include "fearless" and "daring" when I started my career at the age of 22.

I did not know what "audacious" meant back then: only "brave", "bold", "fearless", and "daring", from which arose "rebel" – yet another bad, negative connotation.

To me, these are all different levels of bad, negative, dirty words.

How Dare You, Rebel!

In my younger days, my parents scolded me and called me a rebel for going against their instructions – not because of bad behaviour, but more due to the fact that I did not take their advice on what needed to be done. To me, that was just a matter of different priorities due to different perspectives.

The same thing happened when I started my career. Some of my colleagues labelled me as a rebel who always loved to make unpopular decisions or go against the say of the majority. Because I do not back down from what I strongly believed in, there were times when other labels were thrown at me such as "bit*h", "arrogant", "rude", "strong-willed", "controversial", and "disrespectful" – some to my face, but mostly behind my back.

I did not like it a single bit, all those adjectives that were given to me. It was mean. And hurtful.

It seemed to me that being brave and bold was bad. Being daring and fearless was even worse. Many elders or people in a position of authority preferred me to just keep quiet, to not voice out my disagreements and objections. It seemed that they only wanted me to obey to their directions, instructions, and expectations. As a woman, I could not and should not challenge the person in authority or stand by my decisions – what's more if that person was a man! Otherwise, I am a rebel!

With these adjectives, it looked to all the world like I was a bad person, going against all others: my parents; my immediate superiors; my colleagues; my culture; my community; and the general beliefs at large.

I was always on the "wrong side"; the odd one out. It made me wonder: **Am** I supposed to be who they expect me to be? To be quiet and ignore my own rights to disagree? To silence my voice? Am I supposed to just wait for the bright, handsome warrior to come "rescue", protect, and fight for me as if I were a damsel in distress like in the fairy tales that we all read in our early schooling days?

I really hated how others had labelled me. But if that was going to be the case, so be it: **I rather be called a rebel** – and a whole lot of other negative labels that come with being "audacious".

Yes, I would rather embrace the former than the latter. Both are negative in my eyes – but **audacious is me!**

Audacious Role Models

Here's the "confusion": I resonate with powerful, audacious women throughout history.

I remembered reading about Empress Theodora from a book that I picked from the state library when I was 12. About 1,500 years back, women's roles were limited to looking after the home, and nurturing the family. It was the men who hunted, worked, brought the food back, and protected the family. Men held most of the top ruling positions; they made the call, they decided. Women were to follow and abide.

Although that was one and a half millennia ago, even my generation (Gen-X) can't see much difference between then and today. I had seen – and still see – how men dictate women at home, in social settings, and in workplaces. This has been the way for millennials: it became a culture – worse still, a belief. In certain parts of the world, it is scary to learn that it became a curse for women to have absolutely no rights – other than that of bearing and delivering kids. These poor women do not even have a say on how to bring up their kids! Any attempt to voice out or stand up for themselves would very quickly be treated as an invitation to get beaten or punished.

As such, women who put up a fight for their rights and freedom are "highly controversial", "daring", and "strong-willed" – because the odds of winning against men are low, more so in those olden days. At that time, Empress Theodora was probably known as the most influential and powerful ruler in the history of the Byzantine (the Eastern Roman Empire), as she rose to become Emperor Justinian's chief advisor – despite her very humble origins.

Rather than being an "obedient wife", Theodora pushed for reforms to end corruption by public officials; to expand the rights of women in divorce to include property ownership; to give mothers guardianship rights over their children; and to ban forced prostitution, amongst many others. It meant that her name appeared in nearly all laws passed at that time – a role and activity that was usually the prerogative of the man-ruler of the time.

Another phenomenally powerful woman in history that I find myself amazed with is Cixi, the last dowager of China. There are countless stories and dramas about her (I've devoured them all, I believe), and I highly admired her tenacity: on how this wonder of a woman (whose name is pronounced as Qi-hei in Cantonese) turned her fear into infinite strength as she clawed her way up from being a humble concubine to steering the politics of the Qing Dynasty for 50 years (half a century!).

In that era, the empress was forbidden from being involved in politics. However, Cixi strategically planned to grow her power – and stepped in by introducing unconventional policies, rules, and even deciding who could be the next emperor during her time. Her reforms also banned foot-binding: the painful body-deforming tradition that has been the custom for centuries. And on top of that, she had full control of who should be the foreign ally or partners to conduct business.

What an unusual change to the dynasty!

Cixi bore many negative labels behind her title of "Dragon Lady". Aside from being controversial, she has also been labelled as "cunning", "ruthless", "manipulative", and "cruel". Notwithstanding all these, she continued to pursue what she believed would bring good for her people – and she is still today being appreciated as the leader who brought revolution in the modernising of China.

Yet another influential and formidable woman who I strongly resonate with is former German Chancellor Angela Merkel. During her tenure as the first female Chancellor, she was fearless in standing up against Donald Trump by allowing more than a million Syrian refugees into Germany. It did not bother her when Donald Trump called her a "bit*h" and "kraut;" she stood firm and remained fiercely vocal on how to act responsibly towards other human beings.

Angela was also ridiculed by other nations for her strategies to protect the Euro currency, just slightly more than a decade ago. Despite these non-supportive remarks by her counterparts, the Chancellor stuck to her guns. When the British were struggling to save their economy from falling apart in 2010/2011, Angela was already winning accolades as Europe's Crisis Manager for her role in pushing through tough budget controls to stop the Euro from collapsing.

So, who is the clown here: the one who was being laughed at – or the one who started laughing at others?

All these three women whom I adore are truly audacious – quite clearly, if we were to stick to Google's definition. In essence, all of them displayed strong will, were unconventional, and were daring. One thing that stood out so clearly was that all of them were being violently called out with brutal labels; they were mercilessly mocked and ridiculed. Very often, they were seen as arrogant, disrespectful, and controversial.

But none of them backed down, gave up, nor quit! They insisted, persevered, and charged forward based on what they strongly believed in.

And as I look at myself, I see some resemblances in so many ways. The labels that were thrown at me, and how I strived to achieve what I had today, were the same as what these audacious women I admire had to face. Although the scale may be much smaller compared to them, the journey is still the same. There is no difference to the essence we carry with us – I am, after all, audacious!

I'm being labelled – so what?!? I am who I am: I am Audacity!

Audacious Starts From Within

It feels weird. People find these powerful, audacious women impressive – but not when I show up with their strengths.

For me personally, being audacious simply means **having the courage to do whatever it takes to overcome the challenges to achieve the desired outcome.** As simple as that sounds, it can be a massive challenge for many. The thought of doing whatever it takes can spark off many justifications and excuses about why this or that cannot be done. So easy to say – not at all easy to be done!

But prior to doing and creating the desired result, most people do not realise that audacity actually starts from **within**. What is more important for me, being audacious means knowing who I am inside and **embracing it wholeheartedly** – being able to see my own truth, accepting my weaknesses and failures, and continuing to work on myself onwards, forwards, and upwards!

I am a firm believer of **"What goes on the inside, shows on the outside."** – in other words, our outside world is a reflection of our inner world. When pondering upon my journey, I became truly audacious when I was able to overcoming the shame, fear, and adversity.

Each and every one of us can closely relate to our strengths. We love to remember our successes. Certainly not the weaknesses; given a magic eraser, many would want to choose to erase the failures in their lives. To embrace the "whole" of us can trigger alarm bells. Ultimately, who wants to acknowledge oneself as "less perfect", since weaknesses and failures are seen as "bad stuff"? That makes it extremely tough for many to do. Easier said than done – a real mission impossible for many!

Whenever I am confronted with struggling times, stressful events, and strained moments throughout my journey, I realise that I need humongous courage to conquer the demons within me. The inner voice and negativity that were caused by past mental, emotional, and physical negative events would very often be my biggest critic. And it is through these experiences that I then come to appreciate what audacious really means – or at least, to me personally.

Coming face to face with what could be felt as **painful** requires audacity too. The more pain there is, the bigger the chunk of audacity needed. Many people choose to hide, avoid, and ignore painful emotions; they'd rather not experience it ever. For example, after going through heartaches from a painful breakup, some decide not to get involved in an intimate relationship ever.

Or simply, it is the fear of experiencing the pain itself that could stop someone from pursuing a dream too. Another example: "feeling" the pain of being mocked, teased, or reprimanded from a failure triggers the fear of failure. Hence, this person preferred to stay in her/his/their comfort zone, to only do things that s/he/they can achieve comfortably.

Some choose to indulge in instant gratification such as alcohol, drugs, excessive eating, working overly hard, or shopping. Others may just sweep their feelings under the carpet.

I learnt that it requires so much more strength and courage to handle pain and other negative emotions such as grief and frustration. At the time of writing this piece, I had just lost my furkid aged 7 years and 2 months, whom I treated exactly like my own family member, like my son. Losing him to osteosarcoma turned my world upside down.

It was impossible for me to mend the pain – and for a moment, I had reacted in such a way that I shut away from everyone. I did not want to go home, because each and every corner of the house reminded me of my furkid. I did not want to go to any places that I had brought my furkid to, because I knew it would drive me insane, missing him so badly. I avoided looking at any other pet dogs. I cried; I grieved. I refused to accept that my furkid was gone – because it was just too hard for me to accept. The pain… was beyond description.

Being audacious meant that I looked into the pain and acknowledged it, allowing myself to feel, grieve, and cry it out – then taking steps to face what is reality again. I gave permission to myself to have time to heal – and am now able to go back home, visit places where we spent time together, and accept the presence of another pet dog – all of which required enormous amounts of strength.

You see, we can all continue to avoid all these negative emotions and pain. That is easy. To see the truth of what the reality is; to understand what is the cause of the pain; and to take the necessary steps to address the emotion – these seriously involve immense strength, and are far more challenging. I will say that only an audacious person will able to cope with the entire self, wholly and completely. Therefore, my meaning of audacity expanded to include "being confident, daring, and strong":

- Confident enough to know exactly the purpose of our being and doing. It is only through continuous working on our heads and hearts will we then able to build unshakeable confidence to be our authentic selves and strive forward;

- Daring, being brave, and being prepared to face whatever consequences or repercussions that may come with the decision that is made; and

- Strong enough to see a defeat or a fall as temporary, and then rising up again. This includes being strong enough to apologise when there is a need for it. Not necessarily because you are at fault – but because you have the strength to allow the other party to "win" to achieve an outcome that we want. Or to put it plainly: having the ability to empathise with what the other party has, and how to help ease the situation, behaviour, or reaction.

All the above means "audacious" to me. It spells for authenticity, courage, inspiration, strength, and unconventional. As my courage, confidence, and capacity grew, they enabled me to continue creating the result, the future, and the life that I want. I know exactly – and believe with unwavering belief – that I am, I can, and I will be able to do exactly that – because I know I am always getting better, always more, and always further to go further.

The Audacity in Me

by Bavani Periasamy

When I was first asked to co-author, I did not think much about it. I said yes because it was with a group of ladies whom I know – and I know to some extent we all have the same mindset or wavelength. Or are equally crazy in the head with some of the things we do.

But when it came to actually writing, I was stumped. Like really stuck. Not only my fingers were jammed, my brain froze too. You may wonder why – because I have never ever used "audacity" to describe myself. It wasn't necessary. Anything at all that I do, I think was audacious.

So I thought: "Why not ask the people around me, those who know me well?" So, I asked a few friends – and all said that "audacious" would not be the word that they use for me. Or at least, not the first few words; maybe the last few, said one friend. Another friend looked at me from top to bottom and said: "You? Audacious? Far from it…"

Now this was getting frustrating – and I had to ask back: "What do you think of when I ask about being audacious?" And almost all said: "Thick-skinned, bold, and vocal!"

Again, I'm stuck: I have a chapter to write – and here I am nowhere near audacious at all!! So, I decided to ask another important person whom I thought should know me very well – after all, she gave birth to me. I asked my Amma, as I knew she would give it to me straight, no sugar coating. My mum, being an English teacher, took a moment and said: "It depends on context and how you look at it. If it's about being thick-skinned or disrespectful, you are not. But if it's about a willingness to take bold risks, about speaking up to what matters – then yes, you are."

The Ammas of the world always knows best – and so did mine. This gave me a perspective that I never thought off, as I never saw myself that way. So I started new conversations with my friends – and true enough, the feedback this time was different. This gave me the space to reflect and review on a lot of things about myself. And I came to a decision: **yes, I have audacity in me**!

There are two parts to this, so let me start with the one that was maybe obvious to some – but not me. Yes, I do speak up. I'm usually quiet (though many don't agree with this, and will say I'm a social butterfly).

But I am a social butterfly when the role I am in *expects* me to be one. Otherwise, I'm at a corner tending to myself. There have been times when I spoke up over the last few years – especially when there were issues/challenges that needed me to make a stand, be a voice to groups I am in. During those moments, I feared nothing, and made my stance known. I questioned when I needed to – and I said a big "NO" when I needed to.

There are times when I have been bullied – especially when I am the rare female amongst men in the group that I am in and my voice is dwarfed by others. Even then, I still make sure they hear my "NO" clearly – for I believe that I have the responsibility to speak up because this has been trusted upon me. If not for me, I need to do this for the people I am with.

At the same time, I realise I also have made bold decisions in life. I quit my first job after four years plus of being in a toxic workplace. You may wonder why I stayed that long. Well, it was my first job, and I didn't know better. I thought that was what it was like for everyone. Everyone had Monday blues, everyone worked long hours, and everyone hated work. I checked all the boxes so I thought it was normal.

One day, due to an incident at the workplace, I just decided to submit my resignation without telling anyone, or discussing with anyone – and definitely with no new job waiting, because I had not been looking for one. There was a whirlwind of activity in the office to convince me to stay on, because I had been the longest staff there at that point in time, and too many things were managed by me. I stuck to my decision and left the office after 30 days with all my stuff and no new job.

I think this would have been one big step in my life where I shocked everyone, because I usually am not seen as risk taker. However, when it matters, I do it. There have been instances where I have walked out, or made it known that I would walk out if things did not change. Of course, these happened when I was within small groups of people, never really seen by the outside world about me.

Perhaps, that's why many didn't see the quality of "being bold and willing to take risks" in me.

That's one part of me that I have realised recently. Now, here is another part one which surprised even myself, which I never gave much thought about it till recently.

If there is one part of me that I can strongly say is The Audacity In Me, it would be the fact that **I'm Audacious and Tenacious about MY DREAMS!** I'm ruthless – and have bulldozed my way through this for the last 7-8 years at least.

Remember I mentioned earlier that I worked in a toxic workplace? I am one who is truly lucky; the stars aligned beautifully for me when I also got to work in a place that was so harmonious.

It was like I have experienced hell versus heaven.

Gratitude was one component that I experienced at the workplace. It changed how I look at people and things and situations. I used to be the one saying: "Oh dear, why is this happening to me!?" and "Oh man, I didn't get that sale!" However, my two former bosses – Jonathan Low and Raymond Phoon – helped me see that there is always something good if I really looked at things differently. There are learnings from things that happen; there are a lot more things that are working right in my life while being wrong at work.

This element of being grateful and appreciative made a huge change in me. As I did admin and coordination work, I started to share more on gratitude on social media. I must say that I got coached too well, inspired too much, and definitely empowered too much that I gravitated to being someone who didn't have an inch or ounce of belief in her; I was just someone who shares a lot on Gratitude.

Because I got highly empowered, I started to ask many questions to myself:

- What if one day, I too can speak on stage like the rest of the speakers?

- How nice would it be if one day I can speak about Gratitude to people and let them see the magic in it?

- What if one day I too could be MAPS President? (Now, I thought that was possible when I was in my 50s – because by then, I would have had the wisdom and experience as a speaker)

- What if one day I can sit at home and choose what work I want to do?

- What if I can earn money by just speaking?

- What if one day everyone knows me about The Speaker for Gratitude?

So many questions and so many dreams of what can be possible for me – and by then I knew deep inside me that all this is possible one day. Not today, as I am still an infant in this industry – but one day…

Guess what? Most of it came true – some so much earlier than expected. Though I rejoice what I have come to achieve, not all came easily.

I had to fight with my inner voice and demons. Why?

- Because I was told it would not work.

- Because I was told I had no big dreams! After all, who speaks about Gratitude when the "in" topics are Sustainability, Digitalisation, Women in STEM, Creativity (it seems Gratitude is an easy way out from the REAL topics), etc.

- Because I was told I was not good enough to be a leader since I am not assertive.

- Because I was told that not many Indian girls get to go far, as they have other priorities.

- Because I was told that I didn't have a proper job like many others in my family, who had "proper" careers (like doctors, engineers, you know the rest…) whereas I'm "just" a speaker who does work occasionally and gets paid for that but with no real solid monthly salary.

- Because I was told that I was not good enough – which, incidentally, was also why I was still single.

And so many other Because-I-was-tolds.

I stuck to my dreams: **It's Gratitude or nothing**.

Other than Jonathan and Raymond, I have a good friend who I consider as both a mentor elder brother:

Jegatheeswaran (Jega). One day, he sat me down because I voiced out my insecurity about the topic I wanted to consider as my niche and expertise. He asked me one question: "Can you see yourself talk on creativity or innovation or any other topic that you think of as the 'in' topic of the day?" And I knew immediately, it was a big "NO". It was only Gratitude that I could see myself championing – and that is what it is going to be, which firmed up my decision.

I sometimes recall that whenever I introduce myself and speak about what I do and what I speak on, some people give me this bewildered look of amazement. I guess it's not every day you hear someone who works on "gratitude". Some asked me if there were people who paid me to do work on that area. Some asked if there was a market for it. Some even asked me: "Why 'Gratitude'? Why not something relevant that organisations need?"

WHAT!? Who said we don't need a spoonful of "Gratitude" in our life and at work!?

This made me mad – and even more determined to push this agenda of mine. Keep talking about it. Keep writing about it. Keep reminding people about it. This is important – and I knew that deep down my soul. I kept going, even when people had doubts about me and threw suspicious glances at me and my gratitude.

During the chaos and confusion of the COVID-19 pandemic, I took it in stride and started speaking more. I had a bit more time on my hands anyway – or so I thought. I offered to do free sessions for people who were "stranded" and "troubled". I was helping to apply gratitude to where it could be applied – or at least, I just provided a space for people to pour out. The biggest surprise was to come; the THR Raaga radio station and telco Digi ran a joint campaign to recognise local heroes – and I was nominated because of my "Mastering Gratitude" sessions. I knew then that Gratitude was right for me – and that there was nothing else for me to champion.

Now, I am even more determined to do better, and have come up with a range of merchandise to help me spread my message. You see, by speaking and writing, I can only reach out to so many a day; with my merchandise, I can always remind more people why Gratitude is important, as it helps us move on – especially when we are in tight and difficult situations.

As I do my coaching – working with unemployed graduates, stay-at-home mothers, and single mothers – I realise that many* are stuck in places that they don't want to be. Some are stuck in marriages/relationships that are not healthy; some are staying at a job that they are not happy with; some have to look for a job they don't want because their family pressures them to.

*(I am making a general statement here; it does not apply to everyone.)

I wish that there was a magic wand that I could use to sprinkle some hope, faith, and magic all over people – so that they have the audacity to speak up, to stand up for what's right, and to make bold decisions. As I write this, I realise that we all have it in us – we just need to step up to it.

Waking Up Your Audacity

by Freda Liu

AUDACITY: a willingness to take bold risks.

Everything about this word is frightening to say the least. What got one woman to ask five women to co-write a book, some of whom have never written a book before? That takes audacity. What does it take for six women who have never worked together to attempt working together? It takes audacity.

Let me break down that definition of audacity, "a willingness to take bold risks". Maybe the word "**bold**" scares you. For a person leaving an abusive relationship – that's bold. For a person who takes night classes in addition to a day job – that's bold. For someone who does three jobs to get out of poverty, that's bold. Anyone who takes ANY step to change the status quo is exuding boldness in my books.

The problem is we start comparing ourselves with people who have "arrived" in our eyes, and then we think it's impossible to do what that person does. I look to a lot of people for inspiration, and I like to read between the lines of what they have done and achieved; what they do when no one is watching, when there's no applause. There is always a lot of blood, sweat, and tears not captured on a Wikipedia page.

Lilly Singh is a Canadian comedian, actress, former talk show host, and YouTuber of Indian descent. When she first started out on YouTube, she would post content out twice a week consistently for years, not knowing – or maybe in her case, knowing – what the outcome would be. Her YouTube videos gained traction – and suddenly, she was an "overnight" sensation. As I write this, she is only in her early 30s, having started out in her early 20s – a slow but consistent step to success. So hopefully, the word "bold" now doesn't scare you as much.

Introspection and Self-Awareness

Let's look at the other word, "willingness". This is probably the tougher part; most of us are not willing to take the next step. I have met many people who are not willing (and they wonder why they have not gotten far): people who are not willing to leave a toxic relationship, because it's "better" than not being in a relationship; people who jump into a new relationship immediately, and wonder why they never last;

people who stay in a job that's "secure", even though they are dying inside to try something new; people who are not willing to start a new venture because they feel they're too old or too young.

Where does willingness begin from? I believe it begins with introspection and self-awareness: the ability to tune in into your thoughts, feelings, and actions.

When something is not sitting right, do we stop to dig deep?

At the tail end of my marriage, the last thing I was looking for was another relationship. I remembered someone saying to me that I'd better look for someone while I was still "young" – as if that were the only basis for someone to want me. In this particular case, self-awareness also meant choosing the right friends!

Introspection meant I had to do a lot of healing and necessary growth. I didn't realise it then – but that whole ordeal meant I needed to turn my mess into my message. My son needed to see someone turn out "victorious" from the situation, so that he could also learn from it.

The "boldest" risk I could think of at that time was – first and foremost – spiritual alignment; i.e., having to fill a very empty cup. The next thing I needed to do to continue lifting my spirits was to make self-care a priority. Exercise and choosing the company of the right people were crucial – friends who would encourage me, and hold my hands.

In the area of exercise, it started with my first 10K run; I believed that if I could do this, I could do anything. I needed to build my courage again. The 10K later became a half-marathon – and finally, a marathon.

Writing a book, then, is a new challenge. What went through my head? Doubts and fear – just like for everyone else. But guess what: nobody told me to my face that I couldn't do it. My train of thought nowadays is: "Will I hurt anyone by doing this? Will I die or bleed from doing this?"

Really, that's what usually gets me started on anything nowadays.

There have been many things that I started which never stuck: singing lessons; DJ lessons; guitar lessons; and pole dancing(!). I'm glad I tried it – and hey, maybe I'll revisit them again one day... I now look back on these things as great experiences and learnings – and laughter!

Role Models

I find the journey of being audacious is one of looking for role models and mentors (they may not know you, but you can read about them in books). I look for people who inspire me. Maye Musk – mother of Elon – is a successful woman in her own right, having modelled for 50 years, on top of being a dietitian and having written books.

She became CoverGirl's oldest spokesmodel at age 69, which one news story reported as "making history". At age 74, she was the oldest *Sports Illustrated* swimsuit model – proving that it's never too late to start, and that it's not over until it's done.

In my last book *Life's A Stage*, I talk about the life stages and how we're really on the stage of life. I have been preparing for this life stage over the last 10 years, where my son is heading overseas soon – and I am thinking of my next life stage. How do I stay inspired? Again, the answer is role models.

Oprah Winfrey has always been used as an example, due to the many obstacles she faced growing up as well as those encountered during her career. Now worth billions, she became a millionaire at 32. Her audacity to be the youngest black woman with her own talk show meant she broke the mould when it came to gender, age, size, and race.

Early in her career, Winfrey worked on a failed news show, and was demoted from her primetime co-anchor role. However, the host's empathetic style later found traction, which in 1986 saw her gaining the talk show that rocketed her to international success: *The Oprah Winfrey Show.*

After a quarter-century of success with her talk show, Winfrey's OWN network was written off as a failure by many when it initially struggled to build a viewership or turn a profit. By making a number of changes – such as redesigning the programming, and collaborating with other creators – the popular host was able to turn things around.

And the network still stands strong to this day.

There have been many things written about the Queen of American talk shows – and instead of looking only at her successes, we need to look at the valleys in between, because those comebacks required audacity; what seemed to be small moves put her on a different trajectory – and every move was a bold move.

Another woman I admire immensely is Arianna Huffington, because she's also a former journalist and author. We all know her largely for starting *The Huffington Post* (which is now *HuffPost*) and Thrive Global. Over the course of researching her, I found out a couple of audacious moves she made which oddly she hasn't talked much about. Here's a snapshot of those highlights for me:

- Originally from Greece, Huffington moved to the UK to attend Cambridge at 16. From 21 until 30, she was with the big love of her life – but decided to leave when he didn't want to get married nor have children. That must have been heartbreaking for her – but it was an audacious move to make.

- She wrote her first book at 23.

- For two months, she was the co-host of a late-night talk show on the BBC – only to be dropped two months later (she was 30 at the time).

- She went on to get married at 36, and had her first child at 41 (which I am sure was quite radical at the time).

- She had a radio show at 48.

- She went into politics by pitting against Arnold Schwarzenegger at 53 (she eventually dropped out of the race).

- She started *The Huffington Post* in 2005 at 55, and sold it six years later for US$315 million (RM1.39 billion).

- She left the *HuffPost* Editor-in-Chief role at 66 to start Thrive Global – at the same age.

- And she was selected for the inaugural *Forbes 50 Over 50* – a list dedicated to spotlighting women over the age of 50 who are shattering age and gender norms across every sector of business, politics, the sciences, and society – in 2021, at the tender age of 71 years old.

The Huffington Post became the first commercially-run United States digital media enterprise to win the Pulitzer Prize. Meanwhile, Thrive Global offers behaviour change technology (i.e. science-based solutions) to end stress and burnout; the company and its purpose came about because Huffington herself collapsed at her desk from exhaustion in 2007, and awoke in a pool of blood, with a broken cheekbone – a wake-up call to address the unintended consequences of technology.

And *on top of all this*, she has written 15 books to date.

Inspired yet? I don't think she's slowing down just yet. I think interspersed between all these stories of things that worked, there were also episodes of things that didn't work out, like the love of her life, her two-month stint on TV, her failed political career, her collapse from exhaustion, and her divorce.

She had, however, the audacity to carry on.

Also, pay close attention to the age markers. In case you missed it, she started HuffPost at 55 – when most people are thinking of retiring already (she probably only made her millions in her 60s after she sold it). Her continued vitality in her 70s is likely because she was audacious enough to pursue the things she believed in.

Can't relate? The youngest dragon on the popular TV series Dragons' Den is Steven Bartlett. A university dropout of Nigerian and British descent, he founded Social Chain – a social media content and marketing firm aimed at millennials – which he built from his Manchester bedroom. By the age of 23, Bartlett was a millionaire. Social Chain now has a market valuation of around US$600 million – and the young man himself is worth an estimated £50 million (RM268.77 million).

Bartlett left the company in 2020 to pursue opportunities in blockchain and biotech, and has since launched another two businesses: a Web3 tech platform called thirdweb, and marketing consultancy Flight Story. He's also started a portable podcast called *The Diary Of A CEO* which is already profitable and a huge success.

At the time of writing, Bartlett's not even 30.

In his book *Happy Sexy Millionaire: Unexpected Truths about Fulfillment, Love, and Success*, he wrote: "We are losing ourselves. We're chasing the wrong things, asking the wrong questions, and polluting our minds. It's time to stop, it's time to resist and it's time to rethink the fundamental social blueprint that our lives are built upon." A realisation when he became a millionaire; the introspection and self-awareness to make changes.

(It does help when you're a millionaire, though.)

There are stories of such audacity and audaciousness all around us – and it's not just about the big things all the time; it's not just about millionaires. My late ex-mother-in-law stood by me after my divorce, and continued to live with me to raise my son. That was audacity. She was – and still is – the embodiment of a woman I want to be: a mother-in-law (if I ever become one) who defies all the silly and stereotypical jokes we hear, and inspires me to be a better woman.

When will you start?

These are the stories that inspire me. Sometimes when I am unsure of myself, I take a leaf from these people, and draw energy from their stories of courage. Audacity is **always** the next step I take: not a step I plan to take, nor a step I thought about taking – **it's a step I take regardless**.

Why should you become audacious? Some of us have been here for either a brief time, or perhaps are still stuck here sleepwalking.

It's time to wake up!

It's time to jump the rut and do something different with your life!

Admittedly, some others are living scared. Most of us have been here too; we've all been scared, from time to time. If we allow our fear and worry to imprison us, we may never break free, may never meet our true potential – but if we can find the courage and strength, we may be able to overcome our self-imposed prison to find new amazing success and achievement.

Most of us want something more or something different. You know that you have more in you to give; more in you to share; more in you to accomplish. **Now** is the time to take a leap of faith, and step out.

As you start on this journey with us, remember: **every step you take is bold – if you're willing to do the work...** Be audacious. To quote Lao Tzu: "The journey of a thousand miles starts with a single step."

What's your next step?

Taking the Rough with the Smooth

by Norlida Azmi

Audacity can be a value-laden word. When you first hear someone say he or she is being "audacious", does it evoke positive or negative reactions? Do you flinch – or do you feel inspired? And when you google the word, one of the many definitions you will find is audacity is "courage" or "confidence" of a kind that other people find shocking or rude. (You get the picture.)

So, the range of emotions that is elicited at the use of the word "audacious" – or the manifestation and behaviours of being audacious – is valid. I feel that you must have a high sense of self-awareness so as to decide which side of audacity you want to be known for. When people look you up on LinkedIn, or on another platform/network circle that you are part of, are you known to be an audacious leader, or an audacious person leading a full life? These days your personal branding is a composite of what you put out there – and consistency is key. **Authenticity**.

To be audacious when we are standing up for what we believe is right – either for ourselves individually or for a common cause – that is worthy of my respect. Societal norms also set standards and preconceptions of what is or what isn't audacious. In societies where limits of behaviours are nil to minimal, one can do many things and not be thought of as audacious. The braver amongst us sometimes cheekily push the boundaries to get more meaningful results faster.

Having lived more than 18 years of my life abroad in Singapore, London, Saudi Arabia, Qatar, and the United Arab Emirates, I have had the privilege to see – and at times, experience – different audacious behaviours. At some instances, I flinched – and at some others, I was inspired. One of those was when I was in Riyadh in the earlier years before there were more liberal measures for women. I was inspired by them, where – given the limitations – many pursued higher levels of education up to doctorates, and – when given the opportunities – exceled in the professions based on the knowledge aspect. As the world thereafter opened up, many women were already prepared to assume senior roles.

That was **constructive audacity: to make the most of what limitations impose**.

During that period, I also worked in an organisation that required me to use the *abaya* – and I was a bit audacious, as I moved from wearing a totally black *abaya* (which is the preferred option) to one full of designs and colours. As the only girl in the family, I was always dressed in beautiful things – and sometimes, in daring outfits. There were never expensive clothes – but my late mother loved clothes, and they got passed on to me. So, when I was confronted to wear only black, I thought I would have fun with it. And the *abayas* there were so beautiful: full of sequins, pearls, and so many ornaments. Though I ventured from the norm, I was still wearing respectable versions of the *abaya*. I was called in and gently reprimanded several times – but I stood my ground, in that I still remained respectful of the customs and decorum required. A simple instance of being audacious. Conviction.

The concept of "audaciousness" has been incorporated in the big word for corporates planning transformative growth – **BHAG** (**B**ig, **H**airy, **A**udacious **G**oal, pronounced "Bee-Hag") – that can excite and energise our people and galvanise employees, pulling them together as a team to achieve bigger ambitions as well as upgrade their desires and capabilities to push and achieve something that wouldn't have been possible without the shared commitment. I was recently involved in a large conglomerate that had seriously high ambitions – and the related work included building a culture to support those audacious goals. We had to relook at our values, the "on-and-off" behaviours, and the change management journey identified potential risks. In that corporate space, at times I felt a tsunami of resistance – and that the best way to stay sane was to remain focused on the outcomes. And to have fun along the way, of course...

(The use of "Hairy", by the way, is not an accident – and that's another element of audacity: if we dare to have audacious goals, we need to be prepared to take the risks; the trick is to find the mitigating factors, and move forward audaciously.)

Bringing audacity closer to home, my daughter Natasha took an audacious journey; she certainly shocked my husband and I when – after almost 10 years in a series of increasingly successfully roles in the investment banking industry in New York – she decided to give it all up, and come back to Malaysia – to pursue the dream of designing bras that empower women.

You should have seen our eyes, though we carried the composure of supporting parents.

As a co-founder of SOKO, I saw her motivation and drive, her struggles, and challenges – and yet she was still demonstrating that audacity of wanting to still pursue her dreams. This journey was in the making then – and is still in the making.

I don't have that audacity – or at least, the audacity in that realm. In the professional space, I am fulfilled in a corporate world, pursuing audacious ambitious actions within it. The point that I am making here is that different circumstances will bring out – if at all – different levels of audacity in different people.

My late father was a very dedicated civil servant, and is a role model for my work ethics. He was audacious in his way of engaging with his people – in that, although he may have worked in a fairly-bureaucratic environment, he did not care for the trapping of hierarchies. Way before it was fashionable to engage with your people with "empathy and humility", he was on the ground, breaking rules. He would visit wet markets spontaneously, and pick up a hose to clean the slabs that displayed the produce. It's not always welcomed – but audacious leadership requires you to be relatable and pragmatic. It's not a lofty word, it's a word that **should** galvanise impactful actions.

My role models at the high-profile levels are generally not wholly in one person but rather instances of that person. I admire Angela Merkel for her audacious leadership: during the 2015 refugee crisis, as other leaders closed their doors, she opened up Germany's borders to migrants crossing the Mediterranean and said: "We can do it." How I admire that woman!

And Barack Obama – who said: "Women deserve equal pay for equal work... I believe when women succeed, America succeeds." Whilst his reference then was to America, as a public ally for gender equity and equality, we could not ask for a better spokesperson.

Former PepsiCo CEO Indra Nooyi, who was raised with no real women role models and mentors, said: "...the more we can break the rules, the better off we're going to be."

That sort of audacity takes the cake!

And as I write this, it makes me reflect on whether I have been audacious enough in moments that matter in my life. I have. I am audacious in pursuing my ambitions. I always knew I wanted to be a career woman – and in many of my speaking engagements to aspiring women leaders, my advice is always: "Marry Right", or "Have the Right Partner". This has always been non-negotiable in that I am audaciously ambitious. The audacity does not lie in wanting to be a CEO, but to be in a position that influences. I don't really believe in organisation charts – and this may be wrong for an HR professional to say, because increasingly, I believe the real power lies in influencing to action.

I attempted to stop working after my second marriage, because my second daughter guilted me by saying: "When I become a mother, I will want to wave off my children when they go to school." I tried, I really did; I immersed in community and school activities – but after a year of going OCD and sorting the kids' clothes by colour and my husband's ties by genre (stripes, animal-themed, colours, and other categories that Home Edit would be so proud of!), both husband and kids begged me to go back to "being you". That was scary for me – to take my foot off the pedal of my career journey – but it felt like a journey worth experimenting. Audaciously alien to me.

I am audacious when in love. Going into my second marriage, we had a lot of naysayers. Most said we would not last three months; one year, tops. Well, 23 years later, we are still married because I was steadfast about who would be I would want to spend my life with, and the values I would respect in a partner. "Love" and "in love" – the audacity to walk out of a non-fulfilling marriage and face any family and social backlash because we dare to love who we choose to love. **Conviction**.

I am audacious as a leader. I started working for an organisation that valued collegiate relationships and lateral thinking, and then moved on to an organisation that was fiercely competitive, where the mantra was: "Second place is fine – but not for me." Both organisations were relatively free of protocol, where titles were not that important. You just did things – and that has shaped me into being more confident and fearless. This, in turn, has allowed me to achieve so much more – but it has also pushed me into pits of danger. However, I am too old to change – and I believe in what I believe and what I do. **Conviction**.

So, on that same path, I believed I was moving forward in a balanced mode. An interesting instance to share was that I was surprised when for a project that was looking for talents for a regional transformation programme, one of the inputs was: "She can deliver – but she may be difficult to manage." I could just hear the word "brassy" be used – I would have preferred "resolute", but such is life.

I realised that as a woman, my more vocal and – perhaps – blunt articulations and aggressive moves could have threatened some of my colleagues. This is because I do believe that I was no more vocal nor aggressive than my other colleagues. I learnt early on that it is important that I can live with myself in what I do – and my validation lies in a circle of people that matter, and not just emotionally but professionally. It would cause a lot of mental stress – but I still got selected, and that experience provided me with wider choices in life.

I am audacious as a woman, as a person.

Going back to the start of this chapter on the range of emotions the word "audacity" evokes, I have to be honest that there is this other side of audacity that irks me. I have seen and experienced audacity that tilts more to the "rude" spectrum – where people have decided to do shocking things that do not add any value to the outcome, and along the way causing harm to other people. And like some words and actions, audacity has been repositioned as desirable – so is it really rude, or we do have to look from the other person's lens as it may be an act of courage? (I can still be annoyed though…)

Which brings me to this book. When this group of audacious women invited me to be part of it – so typically of me, I jumped at it. And then I panicked. And then I went into hysterical giggles and thought: "Here you go again, woman, getting yourself into a pickle!" There are moments as I write that flow like a river surrounded by the great inspiration around me – and other moments where I have that "oh-oh" sinking feeling moments. But the thought of understanding myself more keeps me going – and perhaps some of the readers can relate to our stories and introspections.

Audacity is a big word; **taking actions that are audacious is even bigger**. Make that impact that really matters. **Be your audacious self**.

It's in the Pairing

by *Sharma Kumari*

Perspectives

"… 'the audacity of pessimism'… Only when things look bleak will people get round to doing anything."

These are the words of Sir Mervyn King, former governor of the Bank of England (BoE), during an interview with the *Financial Times*.

With that, I begin my first ever book project.

Why did I even think of starting off with "pessimism"? I did not – just as I did not think I would ever write a book, let alone co-author one with five super-accomplished ladies.

Audacity and pessimism are two ends of a spectrum – yet there must be a sense in pairing them as Sir Mervyn King did. I consider pessimists to be those with a generally negative outlook: hardwired to expect the worst, and unwilling to take risks for fear of failure. They could slip into self-denigrating statements like: "Even if I offered my services, it will not be appreciated – and I don't blame them, as I know I can derail the whole project. Anyway, this project is doomed to fail. Why bother!"

In short, the **naysayers**.

I have had occasional self-doubts spiralling into pessimism, such as when I resisted learning to ride a bicycle because I "foresaw" a painful injury in falling off the bicycle. I also anticipated that no one would be around to help – or if there was, I would be so embarrassed and traumatised to have someone see me such. Too much can go wrong. It is true when they say defensive negativity bias kicks in only to help us remain safe. In refusing to learn cycling, I felt deeply protected from any bicycle-related harm.

By contrast, being audacious means "showing a willingness to take surprising bold risks". In short, the **yeasayers**. Given that I viewed riding the bicycle as hazardous, my audacity must have played a big part when I voluntarily signed up for driving. That meant two months of perilous exposure to reckless speeding buses, menacing lorries, unexpected bikers, horrifying other learner drivers, and vulnerable pedestrians (not forgetting, my insufferable instructor!).

Yeasayers have the grit to turn a bleak situation into a positive one. In Barack Obama's *The Audacity of Hope,* he shares how he was moved not just by the struggles of the people of Galesburg, Illinois but by "their determination, their self-reliance, their relentless optimism in the face of hardship".

Sometimes, it can be tricky to recognise audacity.

In mid-2022, American media reported how a group of parents decried the audacity of the San Diego Unified School District Board in reinstating indoor face-masks for all summer school students. Their grounds were that the school board had no legal authority to do so since neither the state of California nor the health department had mandated this.

However, the Board justified its decision with the county's high COVID-19 hospitalisations and new cases. They decided students had to either comply or to attend Zoom classes instead. A parent and founder of the San Diego Rise Up group called this "…completely atrocious and hypocritical…to be requiring kids to be wearing masks while simultaneously the weekend before, there was an LGBT parade with 300,000 people [unmasked]. The audacity of these officials to be using our children as shields is completely unacceptable."

Audacity to… care? I am not sure I follow – nor agree with – their protest. *As a parent*, I would feel reassured by the

Board's concern for the children's wellbeing – especially since the LGBT parade could have "super-spreader" potential amidst the community. Certainly, strong grounds to mask-up.

Switching gears, notice how naturally I slipped into the "as a parent" outlook. Could I have felt this same protective instinct at a much younger, pre-parental stage?

Eons ago, on a bright sunny morning, I went to school on a Saturday, just like some 300 or so Fifth Formers. The schoolgirl chatter was at an all-time high after a three-month holiday. Our "gang" of four managed to locate each other.

It was results day for the MCE (Malaysian Certificate of Education) examination. I clearly recall the trepidation when the quarter-sized A4 slip was handed over to us, destiny hanging in the balance. Outweighing six other subjects was the grade of one: Bahasa Malaysia (BM), our national language. Failing that meant failing the entire exam, regardless of a string of distinctions. None of the four of us had ever failed the school BM tests; yet, the mere thought of a single-pivot determining our next phase of life was unnerving. Simultaneously, we (said a silent prayer?) flipped our slips. The audacity of **suspense**.

Within seconds, we added our shrieks to the cacophony. We had passed with various "shades" of flying colours. The obvious next step was to celebrate! Wasting no time, we left the school grounds for the last time as students, on two motorbikes. We excitedly crisscrossed the town, enjoying a temporary freedom from studies.

Suddenly, at the next traffic light, two traffic cops flagged us down. I immediately froze with the thought of my parents' ignorance of this adventure. Their tolerance and faith in the motorbike was close to zero. My attention shifted to the traffic cops. This incident instantly dwarfed the earlier anxiety of exam results. We were visibly shaken, unsure about what was going on.

The traffic cops informed us that we had not stopped at the red traffic light. We knew this was not the case, and began to animatedly object to this, all at once. Without technology to prove either way, we were left to plead. None of us had experienced a traffic cop face-off. We shared our anxiety since the day before and the present joyous achievement – even going as far as stating how hungry we were and were now waiting to celebrate over brunch. Nothing. Their deadpan expressions gave away nothing.

Honesty and being nice do not pay. Panic turned to desperation. I decided to shift gears to counter their false accusation. Bracing myself, I asked them how it was that only we were stopped when clearly there was a flow of traffic alongside, and behind us? Surely this confirmed the lights were not red. I thought I had nailed it as I saw them muttering to each other.

They scribbled something – and promptly handed us two tickets. We were told to lodge any appeal at the traffic headquarters. The audacity of **truth** trumped by **abuse of power**.

Deflated, we arrived at the traffic police headquarters where we were taken to a large room. Before us was a stern and very senior looking officer. I am sure our pounding hearts were loud enough for his ears. This was scary. His glare did not ease our minds. Unplanned, my three friends looked at me to speak. The audacity of **fear**.

I explained the situation sequentially to him as I had to the cops, ending with how we deserved the benefit of doubt as we were innocent. I wasn't sure if it was a smirk or a glimmer of a smile I saw on his face. Being all lucked out till now, I wasn't willing to assume anything. He lectured us sternly and warned us to never be seen at his station again. Seriously? We made a dash the minute we were let off the hook.

Later, the four of us fiercely discussed and analysed this incident. It was not uncommon for young bikers to be hauled up for no reason other than to settle with a "gift".

Many succumbed, that being an easier option to the kind of intimidation we had just been subjected too. Choosing to audaciously stand our ground mattered to us, as we were innocent. One does not always win.

The biggest relief for the 17-year-old me then was being spared the repercussions at home. Admittedly, empathy for parents was not on my mind. I shudder when I think if it had been me, the parent, going through this. I can now appreciate either side: the audacity of parents from San Diego to Kuala Lumpur in situations involving children, and a child's fear/embarrassment towards a parent's overly-protective nature.

The Audacity Continuum

My various online searches for the meaning of "audacity" exasperatingly kept bringing this up: "a free and open-source digital audio editor and recording application software… operating systems". The algorithms and cookies had the audacity to bypass my intended search!

The battle between human and machine is endless, and I recognized how we must continue to co-exist. Hence, I re-entered the phrase – this time with "audacity meaning". One definition from the Cambridge Dictionary stated that it is "courage or confidence of a kind that other people find shocking or rude". After reviewing a few more definitions, it struck me that audacity-related words could be arranged along a continuum. This meant mapping them based on a person's emotional intensity against his or her conviction to push ahead to action.

Several associates and friends had often encouraged me to write a book, enumerating the various advantages. I stood firm, assuring them that I knew me better – and that they would be wiser channelling their energy to the right persons. I told them that I am contended in the professional speaking domain.

A couple of years ago, co-author Fu-En and I were both elected Exco members of the Malaysian Association of Professional Speakers (MAPS). Amidst our various other interactions, earlier this year I received a chat message from Fu-En asking me to co-author a book. What surprised me was that it took less than a minute for her to hook me to the idea to write and another minute to agree to do so.

Audacity Continuum Matrix

<table>
<tr><td rowspan="2">Emotion</td><td>High</td><td>Courageous, daring, venturesome, vocal, fearless, bold, outspoken, confrontational</td><td>Valorous, dauntless, risk tolerant, hardy, shocking, disrespectful, rude, impudent, arrogant, defiant</td></tr>
<tr><td>Low</td><td>Aware, feel, observe, know, curious, interested, question</td><td>Believe, piqued, confident, probe, gritty, challenge, frank, spirited</td></tr>
<tr><td></td><td></td><td>Low</td><td>High</td></tr>
<tr><td></td><td></td><td colspan="2">Conviction</td></tr>
</table>

Let's understand this "turnaround" with the AC Matrix. (E: Emotion, C: Conviction)

With Fuen's permission, I share our chat as follows:

Fu-En: I'm actually counting u in, in my next book on "[title]" …6 women authors…Each author 6,000 words. Vy doable.

Sharma: Can. This sounds more doable to me – better. Thanks.

Fu-En: So, I count u in ya.

Sharma: Great!

Her opening words *"actually counting u in"* had a personal appeal – an emotional hook that managed to somewhat arouse my curiosity (Emotion: Low). When she added *"in my next book"* I saw a fleeting image of myself swinging into action and taking the challenge to write. I was buoyed by her confidence in me (Conviction: High).

With her words: *"6 women authors"* I was emboldened knowing that I would be amongst several accomplished ladies. I was excited to learn from their collective experience (Emotion: High). In managing expectations and to further encourage me, she did not just say *"6,000 words"* but added *"Vy doable."* When an experienced book project lead stresses that 6,000 words are very doable, I was now dauntless and up for the challenge (Conviction: High).

The outcome may have been different if Fu-En had instead *asked* if I wanted to co-author the book. That would have presented me with an option to decline. I commend Fuen's audacity in driving this project, and in picking out five other women to collectively share their personal takes on audacity.

Keep Audacity Big

From what has been outlined, we can see that audacity is BIG. Its very core is **boldness**. Take it as a compliment when someone challenges you with: "How dare you?!?" It is a backhanded endorsement of your conviction, and of your ability to stand up for your beliefs.

Whatever other contra-interpretations that may be out there, should not define us nor our actions. This little exercise below should convince anyone of the true calling of audacity.

Begin by reading each of these words individually:

- pessimism;

- hope;

- suspense;

- desperation; and

- fear.

Now pair each of them with "audacity":

- the audacity of pessimism;

- the audacity of hope;

- the audacity of suspense;

- the audacity of desperation; and

- the audacity of fear.

Felt the BIG shift?

Pessimism is our creation, our realism. It stems from a bleak outlook. If unchecked, it will limit our growth, sapping every ounce of our remaining confidence. It's like how even before I cook a meal, I am nervous that it will not come up to the expectations of my guests. I anxiously scan facial cues for feedback. With my low self-confidence, I expect them to not like my cooking, even imagining them making a dash to McDonald's after dinner.

Invoking audacity helps to shake off unfounded fears. It allows the mindset to explore and grow. With regards to my dinner, I can now confidently receive honest feedback for the dinner I prepared for my guests, instead of over-thinking the entire evening on what the "verdict" would be.

In his book *The 48 Laws of Power*, Robert Greene wrote: "...Any mistakes you commit through audacity are easily corrected with more audacity." As such, even if the dinner feedback had gone completely south, audacity will continue to push and motivate us to improve until we are satisfied.

Audacity in the right direction, too, will attract apathetic perpetrators.

They will challenge us with: "How dare you?!?"

Respond: "How? I dare with audacity."

To be, or not to be...
AUDACIOUS!

by Syireen Rose

WHAT WOULD THE WORLD look like without audacity?

I never really looked up, or ever thought that there was an existing movement or possibly a new science in leadership known as **audacious leadership** – until recently... Up until taking up the challenge of writing several chapters about topics close to my heart, I didn't know that being audacious was a natural and notably well-placed feature in the path of leadership. As such, I am pleased to share how I have been on this path from way back when, before I knew it was possible – because since the onset of my journey, all I gained from it is to have been labelled as a "rebel", "loose cannon", "unbecoming", "emotional", and – mostly – "unworthy of my cause".

If this sounds familiar to you – or it IS YOU – read on. You are probably on a path that is rarely trudged on: a path of audacity, becoming unfamiliar, almost unknown, and mostly unwelcomed – merely for being a determined-tenacious-forthright woman.

Today, at the time of writing, everyone I know is talking about sustainability and about being a changemaker. Changemakers are currently seen as key players in the industry who are taking bold steps via trainings, proposals, innovations, and implementing good work for change to gradually happen. I like it – and I love being with changemakers who all fuel me with hope and anticipation. I am in awe of what is possible because of the movement. I support it – and yet, I struggle with it because I just don't see myself fitting in because I am a tad bit impatient.

I believe that for change to happen, there must be the willingness to take bold risks, both in speech and action, and this is an absolute but **necessary unpopular** path – something I am increasingly willing to BE because I have proven that such leadership, in all its audacity, creates ripple effects of change. I read a blog by Ricky Nowak, a speaker and a coach, that **the intent of audacious leadership is not fanciful, but purposeful** (which I agree with wholeheartedly). Then she went on to say that **audacious leaders are open to getting the best results through honest collaboration and compromise. To do this, they exercise humility to allow communal success and network growth.**

The latter doesn't sit well with what I view as audacious – and I'll tell you why.

The shortcoming of a word is the simple fact that it is merely letters stringed together. It has absolutely no meaning whatsoever until the language, the culture, the people speaking the word give it meaning. Alas for "Audacity", the word has been corrupted with negativity by the speaking population that recognises it as less savoury.

Give it a shot! Close your eyes and imagine an audacious person. Do you like that person you see? How come?

Having said that, **I** like it – and I am a stand for Audacious Leadership, by my definition. I am simply in love with audacious individuals. I'm not saying they don't irk me or rub me the wrong way, sometimes – yet, I admire the courage, the boldness, the brilliance, and the absolute beauty that exudes from the authenticity of their strength and integrity. Every audacious person I know stands in integrity – and it's a tough act to follow. It's often misinterpreted – but when the word Audacity is understood as "generous", "kind", "abundant", and "strong", the sight of audacious leaders will take the favourable shape as I understand it. Still, it is just a word so it can be everything that you allow it to be for you.

In a TED Talk there was a statement by a speaker that sounds something like this: "…In the lack of confidence, we see arrogance." So, what could we be lacking when we view Audacity in the most negative light? Why can't we reframe audacity as positive?

My stance has always been about getting things done. I'm somewhat of a go-getter, whereby I make decisions and I act on it. Sometimes I succeed, and sometimes I fall short of my goals. I am never shy to acknowledge my flaws – just as much as I will never shy away from declaring my strengths. I wear both my shame and my glory like badges of life on my chest. If I was Tarzan, you'll hear me thumping my chest across the jungle I swing from. My approach may be somewhat unpopular; and yet, the outcomes are often celebrated as wins – though not always credited to me.

So, who cares if I am popular or not? I show up and I get things done! Do I sound arrogant? I honestly don't think so. Instead, to me, my declaration sounds like a fact that is furiously uncomfortable to many – because I choose to believe that I have the right to be proud of my accomplishments. I believe in all audacity that I deserve to take pride in my efforts, whether I win or not! Yet, it is a profoundly unpopular approach to being proud of myself when placed in a culture where having humility and a demure-like personality trump the cards laid on the leadership tables.

We need to change this! There are many girls out there who deserve better, and whose brilliance are drowned by unnecessary naysayers.

I used to get seriously affected and hurt by accusations and labels that were hurled at me, when the only intention of my every action was always about making a good change. I used to think that it was unfair, and almost always whined and allowed myself to BE the victim. I felt dagger after dagger thrust into my back – but when I glanced over my shoulder, it seemed that everyone was cheering me on. It was a confusing time: to be entrusted with responsibilities which everybody expects me to complete – and yet feeling betrayal at every corner.

What changed for me was deciding not to glance over, but to make a complete turn and stare back at everyone to their faces. Confrontation, in my opinion, is part of audacious leadership – because it takes a lot of courage to stare into what you don't like. And as appalled as I was, I acknowledged that what I truly saw were mirrors. Mirrors can't lie; they can only show you your reflection. I learned quickly that what I liked in the mirror staring back was everything true about me – and that what I didn't like was also everything true about me.

I immediately swore an oath to myself that these are the mirrors (things I don't like), that I will work hard on not

BEing. Although, the daggers stayed as reminders, and I bled less – I grew thicker skin. I'm starting to believe that I am an ancient crocodile whose skin is simply impenetrable. The Malay people term this as *"Masuk bakul, angkat sendiri"* (a proverb meaning "To blow your own trumpet") – yet crediting the self every now and then can be quite liberating and audacious.

I took in, digested, and regurgitated the lessons – but most importantly, for things to change, FIRST, I must change. When I decided to take small steps towards being a better version of me, I peeled through my layers of fear, worked on my courage, and watched life shift with small positive ripple effects. We attract what we give, and we can only give what we have. So, work on having a better you to give. Leadership is to be in service.

Ultimately, my conversation is uncomfortable for many who have talked their heads off but never truly crashed and burned, stood in the heat, took the blame, and then rose from the ashes as a committed leader. And lo and behold, the definition of Audacity is: "Boldness or daring, with confidence that disregards personal safety, conventional thoughts or other restrictions."

Look around us. In all honesty, who amongst us and how many of us are willing to take up audacious leadership? Who do you know will truly step up, knowing that s/he will make unpopular decisions and experience crashes and burns before truly rising from the experience, because only learning makes us better?

Yet, no... this was never my dream. I never wanted to lead nor to be audacious. I am a reader and I am a writer; I love my secret getaway caves where I huddle with my book and a cup of coffee to be lost in my blissful life. Then one day, I crawled out of my cave – and did not like what I saw. I wanted a better world than how I left it and so I got to work. I have not looked back.

So, what have I done?

Audaciously Blunt

I make no excuses for BEing honest. I trust that **truth** likes it too. I feel that feedback is important – and there is a HUGE difference between giving feedback and casting displaced character assassination (as is commonly practiced). Maybe honesty is twisted – but I'd rather come forward than succumb to sleepless nights.

I am assuming that in most Asian communities, we are expected to sugar-coat, beat around the bush, and pepper conversations with niceties. They call it manners; I call it a waste of time. Did that sound arrogant again? Or did that sound like reality? I'd vote for the latter. I trust that the truth likes what is real and not what is imaginary.

I'm not saying that being honest don't create mishaps – but I feel it is easier to rectify that than saying what you sorta-wanna-say-but-are-not-really-saying-what-needs-to-be-said – because we are afraid that someone's heart will break (or as we say here in Malaysia: *#isentap*).

Recently I was told I invalidated someone while giving feedback. I was coached that "feedback's" best friend is "clarifying questions" – unless the receiver is too defensive to see clarity through the muck; hence, it was what it was. I did what I had to do – and so did she. Then I left it at that.

A necessary unpopular stand – but I am who I am: **Audaciously Blunt**.

Audaciously a Bulldozer

I don't remember any of my superiors enjoying this part of me. Although they reluctantly acknowledge the benefits of it, they just don't enjoy it when I show up audaciously bulldozing.

Although I recognise the importance of democracy and getting the majority to agree in order to make decisions or get things done, when the definition of majority is 100% in agreement – which never happens in any universe – it gives permission for the folks in charge to create justifications for why things can't get done and for embracing complacency instead.

Yet, change is a constant! Everybody wants better things; everybody likes new stuff and exciting innovations – as long as they don't have to be responsible for it… I'm okay with that – because then, I get to take the responsibility, bulldoze, and get things done.

Not a very comfortable take on things – but from experience, I cannot wait for folks to dwell on issues, feed into the drama, brainstorm, ask permission, brainstorm some more, wait for a variety of red tape to be removed before we begin the first step to success. At the same time, from experience, I know that when I pave the pathway and show the brightness at the end of the tunnel, people get up and follow.

Haish… is that arrogance again? No *lah*; that's just experience. Like it or not, I am a bulldozer because I like getting things done. I especially love success that I can share with others.

A necessary unpopular stand, but I am who I am: Audaciously a Bulldozer.

Audaciously Teaching, Sharing, and Revealing

When I began my teaching journey, I was overzealous and excited to share what I knew – so much so that I did not take into consideration the audience, who were young and impressionable. I showcased case studies and shared perspectives; I called on the audience to be critical and peel through worldviews, belief systems; and cultural bias – and I came out of that being labelled a racist. Oops!

What happened?

I guess I will never know – but a decade after the incident, the student who started the movement against me looked me up on Facebook and apologised; she now sees the importance of perspective in learning.

Still, I passionately believe in the power of knowledge sharing – and I believe that everybody holds varying thoughts of a single phenomenon. So, no matter how imbalanced the world is, I believe we need teachers to invite people to think. We need to know how to see, hear, and heart what is different in us – yet is so uniting that it makes us 100% human.

My mentor says that thinking is the hardest thing to do, which is why so few embark on it. I found that statement so disheartening – because if we don't think and learn, how do we grow? So, I insist that everybody should be given access to knowledge, whichever stage they may be at in life: personal, professional, or spiritual.

We are not cultivating haughtiness knowing that we give what we give; rather, we see it as a humble invitation for others to step up, wipe off the grime, and reach for excellence. We are all brilliant creatures with gifts; why keep your magic locked up in the attic for dust to rest and the spiders to party?

So, when I receive value, I teach; I share; I reveal with all audacity – and I can't wait for folk to be ready to begin giving what I know and what I have learned. Knowledge is free for the taking – and I am a willing giver: take it or leave it, knowledge is forever present.

A necessary unpopular stand, but I am who I am: **Audaciously Teaching, Sharing, and Revealing**.

.

.

.

.

.

What would you like to be? In all audacity, I sincerely hope the answer is: **AUDACIOUSLY YOU!**

CHAPTER 2
How to Be Audacious

Listen to Your Audacious Heart

by Fu-En Yee

I am a strong believer that "how" comes naturally when we know who we are, know what we want, and know why. Each and every one of us is unique, because our values, beliefs and definitions are different: what fully works for me, may only work partially, work a little, or even not at all for you.

There are few of us who are born audacious. Most of us develop the traits of being audacious due to the circumstances and experiences that we had: we learnt to be audacious.

As I lay out how I got to be audacious, you need to ask yourself if you truly want to be audacious – and to be ready to accept audacity as part of your being. Note that "wanting" to be audacious, being "willing", and being "ready" to embrace audacity are three completely different considerations!

One can want to be audacious, yet not be willing to be audacious. If you are not willing, then you are far from being ready. So how do you know if you are willing to be audacious? Below are a few questions for you to honestly reflect upon:

- Are you willing to have mean labels being thrown at you (and remain ok with it)?

- Are you willing to defend your decisions, even if everyone else is against you?

- Are you willing to do whatever it takes to do things that are completely different?

If you answered "Yes" to all three questions, then **you are willing**. Otherwise, you are not. No matter how much you want to be audacious, you will not be able to only for one main reason: you care about what others think, see, and say about you!

In other words, you constantly need other people's approval or validation.

The Shameless Me

The most important criteria to be audacious is to be shameless for who we are. Make no mistake: there is a huge difference between being shameless and having thick skin. I see a connection between shamelessness with self-love, and thick-skinnedness with being selfish.

The distinction between the two lies in the intention.

Being shameless means **I am not afraid to be who I am** despite how others perceived me to be. Being shameless signifies that I know my life's purpose and the meaning of my existence pointblank – and that all that I do is serving towards that purpose. Being shameless indicates that I love myself enough to first take care of my own self in this long journey to help more people to build better humanity.

Just as how Empress Theodora was termed "merciless" for having rebels and rivals executed; the truth is that her intention was to secure the kingdom for her husband, Emperor Justinian. Empress Dowager Cixi is painted as "ruthless" and "cunning" in her drive to modernise China; and of course, Chancellor Angela Merkel paid scant attention when being called awful names by Donald Trump when she bravely stood against him.

All these audacious women were shameless because they know downright what were their purpose and intention. How other people see, call, and remark did not, do not, and will not define them. Neither will these stop them from marching forward to accomplish what they had set their mind to.

What others thought was none of their business.

Call, say, and think whatever you want – but I am forging ahead! Because I know myself so well, all the labels just bounced off of me. I did not let these get into my mind, nor did I allow these to affect my beingness. I'd rather preserve my energy for thoughts and actions that bring me closer to my goals.

Didn't these callings and labels hurt? Well, yes! Of course, they hurt! After all, I am just an ordinary human being. I, too, have my pride and ego; I get angry at how the systems in society had conditioned the minds of the public. I get upset when people get me wrong and misunderstand me. Sometimes, I do ask myself: Am I a misfit? I feel disappointed when people cannot understand why I am pursuing specific agenda.

But then, between being misunderstood on a good purpose and being accepted by many yet going against my purpose, I would rather be misunderstood – because I believe the truth will prevail. **This is who I am**; I only live this life to fulfill my purpose. You need to be audacious to do it.

Being thick-skinned, on the other hand, means the person has no regard for anyone else aside for herself/himself/themself. Thick-skinned people are insensitive. They would not be bothered by how others feel, think, or say. To them, those have no meaning. They are indifferent. You can curse and swear about it – who cares?

You can see this attitude mostly in politicians. They give impressive speeches, and even make bold promises. They need to be brave enough to put up the great showmanship. They are courageous in this manner. But then, they are fake. So many promises are left unkept once they get their seat. Are they concerned at how the public curse and swear? Of course not! They only care for their own personal agenda. That is why I associate being think-skinned to being selfish – and that, my friend, is being "notorious", **not** "audacious".

Be Prepared To Obey "Myself" First

Fundamentally, this is one lesson that you must also learn. Yes: **obeying your own needs comes first** – not your parents-in-law, not your spouse/partner, not anyone else.

"What??"

Although you may have this reaction, what you just read is **exactly right. Obey ourselves first**. Take care of our needs first – because only when our needs are met and able to maintain our happiness, calmness, and fulfilment are we then able to love, take care, and serve our loved ones whole-heartedly.

Many years back when I was still serving in the leadership team of a corporate body, I was experiencing overwhelming stress due to work overload. My CEO then asked me to take on additional tasks to deal with the local authorities to help the other colleague – he was foreigner, and somehow, the local authority personnel was giving the colleague a hard time. My heart, body, and mind were screaming: "No!" – yet I just took on the extra work – reluctantly. "Who can manage it further if not me?" I was thinking.

Due to that, I had a major health breakdown – and was on medical leave for 10 days. As a result of not listening and obeying my own needs first, I fell horribly sick, and was unable to perform any of the duties for that period of time.

I was audacious all the while – but in that moment, I had not learnt to listen, trust, and obey **myself**. I could have just said: "No." – because there was more than enough on my plate. Moreover, it was the colleague's responsibility; he should be the one to figure it out and work it out.

But I didn't. I was not my full audacious self – because prior to 2016, I had not learnt what self-love means. I did not know the importance of first obeying myself.

Being audacious starts within.

Stepping Out from Being An Introvert – Temporarily

You read that right.

You are an introvert? I am, too.

Most of my sisters who are part of this project are introverts too.

Being audacious require us to speak up! No matter how painfully shy or seemingly impossible it is for you to be an extrovert, I would like to invite you to just step out from being an introvert for just a very short time, to address what is needed – then you can go back to being your authentic self again.

When you know what you stand for, your conviction will rise above this. Your heart will be filled with so much of energy that you can temporarily jump into an extroverted plane!

Reflect: Have you come across a new acquaintance at a function and suddenly found a mutually-interesting topic that you have so much to share about? You ended up having a long conversation, forgetting the time passing by. Right? At that moment, you stepped out from being an introvert, and became an extrovert – because you were conversing about a subject that you are passionate about.

That's **YOU** being your extroverted self!

If you ask if we can simultaneously be an introvert and an extrovert at the same time, the answer is: Yes, we definitely can! At the end of the day, it depends on how much conviction you have about yourself and about something that your heart holds ever so dearly on to. If it is important enough to you, then speak up! Step onto your extroverted self, and go for it, no matter how small you may think it is! If you have a dream, speak of it passionately – loud enough to drown the naysayers, because nobody ain't gonna to make your dreams come true, except you!

Willing To Be Wholly YOU

"Every failure is a lesson.
If you are not willing to fail,
you are not ready to succeed."

There are three ultimate masteries you need to learn to be audacious: Firstly, being shamelessly you; secondly, obeying yourself; lastly (but not least), step into your extroverted self.

If you paid attention closely, you would have noticed that it all boils down to how much you know yourself – and then owning your true authentic self.

Are you **willing** to do so?

Many people want to be successful; want to be rich; want to brave; want to be audacious. They want to be this, and want to be that. As I mentioned above: "Want to be" and "Willing to be" are two completely different things. "Want to be" is a **thought**; "Willing to be" requires **action**!

Are you willing to be to embrace the whole you – both the awesome side, and the less perfect side?

When you already have concerns about being audacious, it simply means you have worries about not being accepted nor desired by others. You are afraid of being an 'outcast" – or, you are fearful your loved ones and closed ones will no longer care nor love you when you become audacious.

To be honest, it is a fair concern. Since we were born, we grew up being cared for, loved by, and fed by our parents or guardians. In school, we were taught the way to get the praise and attention of others, through acceptance by teachers and friends. We survived childhood, because we have them looking after us.

All along, our brain learnt that we could make it so far by being acceptable to others. The thought of being singled out can trigger an alarm with lots of discomfort – because the brain picked that as endangering our lives. To be shamelessly us is definitely easier said than done, after all!

However, it does not mean that that situation cannot be overcome.

Question your own beliefs. You can start to ask yourself the following:

- Is it true you cannot survive by your own?

- What makes you believe you will be the lone ranger in the journey of being shamelessly you?

- Is it true that everyone will shun you off when you become the **real** you, shamelessly?

- Can you not survive mean labels?

- Can those negative descriptions define you – when only you truly know who you are and what you stand for?

Think and reflect.

Know Yourself Well and Deep

"Great people do things before they are ready."

I resonate with this quote a lot.

I still remember when my grandfather tasked me with being the leader of the family when I was 7-years-old. I was not ready at all – but I took it on, because of the conviction that I had about being the leader rising above the fear and doubts.

We know of dating couples who wanted and were willing to get married – but were just not ready to for marriage. We have also seen married couples want and be willing to have a child – but are not ready to have the child be part of the relationship. Some mothers experiencing postnatal depression. Some couples start to have major arguments about who has to take care of the crying baby at night.

You may want and willing to be the shameless you, to be the audacious you. You may or may not "chicken out", or withdraw if you are not ready for it.

There are many occasions when people do not know what kind of challenges they put themselves into until they step right into it. They think they know themselves, and they assume they are ready for them – because they want to, and they are willing. Just like being newlywed or first-timer parents: once they are in, the thoughts and feelings became completely different.

Most of the people I know thought they knew themselves well – until they were in that scenario for real.

If in your journey towards audacity you experience withdrawal instead of rejoicing, it is a sign of misalignment between what is in your head and what is in your heart. Instead of reacting and cursing at yourself for being weak, take deep breaths, and calm down. You will need to go deeper into yourself – and reflect upon what triggered such withdrawal or resistance.

Remember, facing the negative emotions and finding ways to address them is a huge part of the most important steps in materialising your true self, your audacious self.

At the end of the day, it really depends on how much do you know about yourself; how deep are you willing to go; how strong your conviction about yourself is.

The deeper your understanding of yourself is, the stronger your conviction about your core will be – and the more audacious you can be.

Don't Overthink, Just Do It!

by Bavani Periasamy

When I saw this topic title, I had to think long and hard, as well as think back about my own life: how and when was I audacious? This was churning in my mind for a while, as I tried to find the right elements to share.

I spoke to a dear friend once about toxicity at workplace, when I mentioned that I didn't know how it was that I didn't think much about it when my already-toxic work place was doing things that did not sit too well with me. Today, I can look back and say that many things were not in line with my values and principles, which I still hold on strongly to.

What did I do? I quit – without a new job in place. I was very young then: underpaid, just four years out of college, and with pretty much nothing in terms of cash reserves – but yes, I quit. My friend said: "If that's not being audacious, what do you call that?" Thanks, buddy, for kickstarting the thought process of what else being audacious is about, and how to be audacious.

How is quitting a job without much thought to it nor with a plan in place being audacious, you may wonder? Well, simply said: it's about moving past any hesitation or insecurities you may carry with you. Was it a smart move? Nowadays, I would (probably) say: it's not. But on the other hand, if I did not do it, I would have been forever sitting there for the comfort of job security. Everyone was saying: "Make sure you have a signed job contract before you ever resign."; I didn't even have a job interview lined up yet when I left.

I just decided to be audacious (which, I now know, I didn't realise back then…). I knew I couldn't hesitate too much and overthink it – because I might have ended up just sitting there and compromising the values and principles that I had (and still have).

As I reminisce about that, other incidents pop up in my mind. It's about the playfulness that comes along by colouring outside the lines. I remember once reading what the Dalai Lama said: "Know the rules well, so you can break them effectively." – which to me means that sometimes, some rules are made under certain circumstances, based on certain beliefs and certain rituals, and that we need to know and understand them very well so that we can do what we want – or in other times, understand them to do things in a way that serves us better.

I'm not referring to rules in the eyes of the Law; I'm referring to rules that apply to society from a cultural and religious perspective. I am quite sure there will be some who may not agree with my perspective – and that's OK. This is purely how **I** interpret it, and use it in a way that is useful to myself. One simple example that comes to mind immediately is the fact that in some cultures, there is a belief that you should not cut your fingernails at night. Yes, this is quite understandable from the point of view ages ago in the era when we did not have electricity readily available like we do now. The chances of us harming ourselves were quite high if this activity was done at night – back then.

Another taboo about trimming nails at night that I heard often as I grew up was that it is a form of disrespect towards the Goddess Laxshmi, who is known to be the Goddess of Abundance, Beauty, and Good Fortune – so cutting your fingernails at home at night did not sit well in many families who worshiped the beautiful Goddess Laxshmi. Yet another taboo that I heard was how nails cut at night and thrown out could potentially be used for black magic – which, of course, is not something you and I may be too fond off.

Growing up with many of rules like this has occasionally made me go crazy. Strike that: not *occasionally*; it *had* driven me crazy a lot, 'cause it was absorbed into my belief system. So, I needed to understand these rules, and make sense of it – and yes, I *do* cut my fingernails at night nowadays. Why? Simply because that is a convenient time for me to do so.

I can find myself rationalising to being able to break these "rules" which have been in existence for a very long time.

This is just one simple example of how you can colour outside the lines – but it does take some audacity to go against these set rules by breaking them. Did I sin by doing so? Maybe. But can I live with it? For some of these, my answer is: **Yes, I can.**

As I was writing this piece, I reached out to Dictionary.com and searched for "Audacity" – and this is what it showed me:

- extremely bold or daring; recklessly brave; fearless: *an audacious explorer.*

- extremely original; without restriction to prior ideas; highly inventive: *an audacious vision of the city's bright future.*

- recklessly bold in defiance of convention, propriety, law, or the like; insolent; brazen.

- lively; unrestrained; uninhibited: *an audacious interpretation of her role.*

audacious [aw-**dey**-sh*uhs*] SHOW IPA 🔊 ☆

See synonyms for: audacious / audaciously / audaciousness **on** Thesaurus.com

adjective

1. extremely bold or daring; recklessly brave; fearless:
   an audacious explorer.
2. extremely original; without restriction to prior ideas; highly inventive:
   an audacious vision of the city's bright future.
3. recklessly bold in defiance of convention, propriety, law, or the like; insolent; brazen.
4. lively; unrestrained; uninhibited:
   an audacious interpretation of her role.

Now, something else was screaming at me when I read this: the last sentence, which speaks about being **lively, unrestrained,** and **uninhibited**. It reminds of times when I questioned my own life a decade ago. I was thinking too much about what I wanted to do – and what would the people around me think about it. What would society say? What would my friends think of me? What would their perspective of me be like?

I spent so much time thinking about all this that I forgot to live my life.

It took me a while to realise that I can do what I want, how I want. It took me a *long* while to realise that I would always be emotionally driven and sometimes too sensitive about things around me – and that it **did not mean that I am**

a weak person. I now believe it takes great strength to live a life that embraces all those sweet tendencies (Yes, I call them sweet – and not weak anymore).

I can cry over a drama series and not be embarrassed about it. I know its OK to tear up and break down when the person I am coaching shares stories that are just heart-breaking. I am only human – and I no longer feel the need to hide all this from the world.

Something lecturer and author Brené Brown said in her book *Rising Strong: The Reckoning. The Rumble. The Revolution.* helped me get to this stage. She said: "The irony is that we attempt to disown our difficult stories to appear more whole or more acceptable, but our wholeness – even our wholeheartedness – actually depends on the integration of all of our experiences, including the falls."

I not only had falls, I had a truckload of insecurities, inferiority complexes, and a whole load of emotions bottled up.

I just somehow had the audacity along the way to get lively and get uninhibited.

I embraced my life. I embraced the beauty that life has to offer. I embraced Gratitude, and made it my life's mission to spread awareness about it. The Bavani from a decade ago did not think that people would want to hear her talk. *"Who is she for people to sit and hear? After all, she's just this girl from a small town called Port Dickson…"*

I'm not sure about others, but I have embraced the notion that you need to have the audacity to release the restraints that you have on yourself– the restraints that the society has on you – and move forward towards what you really want.

There is a popular saying that goes: "Whatever you can do or dream, begin it. Boldness has genius and power and magic in it." Although it has been attributed to Johann Wolfgang von Goethe, it was actually a translation in 1835 by Irish poet John Anster of two lines from Part One of the master's tragic magnum opus Faust (do read the about the history of it on Quote Investigator – it's fascinating).

Regardless of the origins, I find them magical – how beautiful these words are! As I type this, I can hear my own father's voice saying what he always has told me since I was a little girl, and continues to tell me up to now: "You can do anything you want – it's whether you want it or not, and whether you believe or not."

Deep down, this is also the reason why I am pursuing my message on Gratitude. I have a dream – and my dream is to help people believe in their dreams using Gratitude.

However, I can't do much if I never moved nor took action. Dreams need action; Dreams need boldness; Dreams need the audacity to push through and get things done. I know I got to take some bold and risky steps – but if I do not, I would not be doing my best in sharing my message. My message will be stuck with me – and that would be selfish of me, if I did not do everything I possibly could to share messages and inspiration on Gratitude.

We all have dreams. We all have beliefs. We all have a purpose – and we all need to be audacious to go after it.

Each of us, in the different roles we play in our lives, whether knowing or unknowingly: we are audacious. We stand up and speak up for what we believe in. We do not compromise when our values and principles are being challenged. We stand firm when we need to, to protect the people we love. We harness great strength from within us to be audacious when we need to step up and do what needs to be done.

If women were not audacious, we would never have had people like Mother Theresa, Princess Diana, Oprah Winfrey, Jacinda Arden, Greta Thunberg, Malala Yousafzai – the list goes on and on.

I also wish to say this: **they are not the only audacious women around.** There are many unsung heroes living among us. Our mothers, our sisters, neighbours, teachers – the list goes on and on. One does not need to be in a position of power to be audacious. We can be from where we are right now. We start with our own selves – and we empower and hold on to other women, other females to also be audacious.

Audacity is in all of us. We hold the power to decide how to be so. We can be audacious and make waves of changes – or we could create a whole lot of trouble.

We choose what we want. We stand up for what we want and for what we believe in.

A Pinch of Audacity,
A Heap of Conviction

by Freda Liu

BHAG: **B**ig, **H**airy, **A**udacious **G**oals.

Most of us have heard of this – usually at the start of January, as we prepare for what's to come in the new year. As I am writing this, I have several deadlines looming ahead (including writing this!) – and I find myself at a crossroad with some impending challenges ahead.

(No, I didn't preempt these challenges.)

Is there a formula for audacity? I will share my thought process – and maybe that works for you too. I wish I could just whip out 10 steps and voilà! We're all audacious!

(I would definitely bottle it, and sell it for a fortune.)

But before we get ahead of ourselves, there are some important points to consider before we take that step towards audacity. Comparison; Self-Sabotage; Persistency;

Consistency; Procrastination; Resiliency – these are some of these values I want to address before we get into the topic of how to be audacious. Let's see if any of these personal stories strike a chord and connect with you.

Comparison

Let's talk about comparisons first. In our quest to be audacious – whatever that means to you – **be aware of your reasons**. We look around at someone else's achievements, and we think: "I'm too young, too old, too fat, too thin…" – you get my drift. We stop before we start. We're comparing someone's middle to our own beginnings.

But you must remember: it's your own journey and timeframe that matter when setting out to achieve your goals.

Instead, turn in the word "comparison", and replace it with "aspiration". Who is aspirational to you? I have many idols and role models – and yes, they include the usual suspects like Oprah Winfrey and Arianna Huffington (who started The Huffington Post at 55). However, I also look up to the one and only Jennifer Lopez. No, I won't be singing, acting, and dancing like her – **yet** – but she has proven capable of evolving and remaining relevant over these decades. I absolutely admire her tenacity – and not only does she have that in spades, she even encompasses all those other values that I'll be talking about.

Saboteur

This leads me to the prickly point called self-sabotage. I'm currently reading this book by Gina DeVee called *The Audacity To Be Queen: The Unapologetic Art of Dreaming Big and Manifesting Your Most Fabulous Life*. In her book, she talks about a coaching client, and her story is definitely something we've heard about or – God forbid – something we're currently doing: being a saboteur to our own life.

DeVee talks about a woman who started her own business, who followed all DeVee's coaching advice – and made such astounding success during her first month in the business. The preceding month, her client was nowhere to be found. The woman called DeVee several weeks later and said that the business was a fluke; that she had gone back to full-time employment (despite not liking it); and that all the money she made had been spent on a holiday (no wonder the business didn't survive the next month)

In other words, self-sabotage.

I went on a Money & You programme years ago, where the facilitator talked about our relationship with money.

Some people have a "drama hook" – and there's always some drama going in some people's lives. After a while, your friends will get tired of giving you the same old advice.

However, let me go a little deeper here. In the case of the woman, maybe it was her observations of her father – who never succeeded in business – that led her to subconsciously believe that it was the same case for herself too.

If you see some patterns in your life that're not helping you, go deeper. If your friends can't help (since they are not trained in that area), work with a professional coach.

Persistency & Consistency

In this world of instant gratification, it is important to remember that **corn does not grow overnight**.

(I don't think they've managed to genetically modify this yet but you get my drift.)

Looking at my own career path, the core of what I do is communication. (Yes, people may know me from radio and TV.) However, I have spent more than three decades working in these fields, together with public relations as well as lecturing (albeit the latter was not for very long). I have covered the gamut of everything communication, and still have to learn new skills and tools like TikTok (or whatever the next flavour of the month may be). It is not immediately comfortable – but yes, I have to learn this, just like how I'd previously done all my work.

Throughout almost all of my working life, I have never only done one thing. There was a bit of money from my many side hustles – but it wasn't a lot of money. In my previous career at IBM, I had a full-time job as a Communications Manager – whilst also working as a news presenter on TV and radio in the evenings and over the weekends.

That sacrifice of my time earned me what was not exactly great money – but most importantly, I never lost the broadcasting skills. Nowadays, we have tools at our disposal like YouTube videos and Spotify podcasts: there is no excuse. What are you willing to be persistent and be consistent about?

The Japanese concept of *kaizen* is about achieving improvements by taking small steps instead of drastic, rigorous changes. Although improvements under *kaizen* are small and incremental, the process brings about dramatic results over time. If you meet an old friend that you've not seen for a while, do you see *kaizen* in their lives? More importantly, will you be able to see the *kaizen* in **your** life?

Procrastination

Now, let's go to an old favourite. The path of least resistance is always the best. (Sleeping is always better, trust me.) Watching the latest movie on Netflix is better than writing this chapter!

Is it even possible to overcome procrastination?

I do have a little skill though. Below is a little prompter that keeps me going.

	URGENT	NOT URGENT
IMPORTANT	**QUADRANT 1** **REDUCE** Deals with crisis management. Reduce time spent in this quadrant by doing more work in quadrant 2	**QUADRANT 2** **SCHEDULE** Involves future planning through strategic thinking. Requires initiative. Spend more time here
NOT IMPORTANT	**QUADRANT 3** **DELEGATE** Empower team by assigning tasks in this quadrant. Enable your team to do independent decision making.	**QUADRANT 4** **DECLUTTER** Eliminate tasks that do not align with company's mission and goals. Learn to say no to them

It's popularly known as the **Eisenhower Decision Matrix**: a productivity, prioritisation, and time-management framework designed to help you prepare a list of tasks or agenda items by first categorising those items according to their urgency and importance.

What's the most important quadrant you should look at? Well, most of us are firefighting in Quadrant 1, spending time on the important and urgent. (And yes, those things happen.)

However, if you spend more time looking at Quadrant 2, you might just kick the procrastination habit for good. An example of a Quadrant 2 fit in my life is my health. My father died two months short of his 60th birthday, which made me look at what possible health challenges I might have. Guess what: if I don't watch what I eat nor exercise today, it won't make a difference tomorrow. However, if I don't watch what I eat nor regularly exercise today, it'll definitely make a difference in 10 years.

I then broke it down to daily habits. It's been said that if you exercise three times a week, you'll see and feel the difference. I knew my own patterns and behaviour best. Three times a week this week will become two times a week – and then once a week – and then, nothing...

Know thyself, I say.

Some people are disciplined enough to do it; I'm not one of them. I knew, though, that I needed to make exercise a daily, deliberate activity until it becomes a lifestyle for me. So come rain or shine, lockdown or no lockdown, I made sure I exercised every day.

That's just one part of my life. What else in your life needs some Quadrant 2 overhaul?

Resilience

This brings me to my next point. In my talks on this topic, I found a connection: setting goals has everything to do with Quadrant 2. I gave you an example earlier on one aspect of life (fitness). If you know about the Wheel of Life, there's anything from eight to 10 elements that fit into the puzzle that is your existence. These elements include:

- Fitness;
- Finance;
- Friends;
- Work/Business;
- Personal Growth;
- Environment;
- Love;
- Family;

- Faith; and
- Fun.

Let me give you two more examples. Let's talk about writing books, and I'll put this under Personal Growth. **Why do I want to do this?** It always comes back to why. I wanted to push myself in this area, and to see if I could write books. Other reasons include enhancing my career and skills set, as well as gaining recognition.

All good and well – but **do I need to write a book?** No.

Will a book help my branding and portfolio? A resounding yes.

Have I ever done this before? No.

Can I learn how to do it? Yes.

The work behind the scenes meant finding a publisher, a deadline, deciding what type of book I wanted to write, followed by the most important aspect of the process: actually writing the book!

And so, I developed a timeline that showed what I needed to do on a monthly basis, a weekly basis, and a daily basis. That was the groundwork – and whenever I got a little lost, jaded, or bored with the mundane process (when no one's around behind the scenes watching you work nor applauding you), I go back to **why** I want to write the book.

The same philosophy applies to every other area in the Wheel of Life.

Now, when doing the "important and not urgent" stuff from Quadrant 2, make sure you celebrate along the way when you have small wins. Otherwise, it can be a long, winding, and arduous road. Take a moment to applaud yourself; go ahead and pat yourself on the back. Give yourself a little reward for every milestone – which can also help you move along as you work through for your own reward.

I am the sort of person who can just work and work and work – and I know that sooner or later, if I don't schedule fun in general, I will lose steam. I used to be that person – and I dare say it was definitely one aspect that affected my marriage. So now, make sure to schedule fun into your life. You decide what it is: trying out a new restaurant; going for a massage; planning (and going through with) a weekend getaway; having a night in with friends to watch a movie together. Remember: all work and no play make Jack (or Jane) a dull boy (or girl).

I have gone into every area in my life and scheduled what's important and not urgent in such a way that it need **never** become urgent in future. Time with my son –

especially up until today, as he approaches manhood before he leaves for overseas – is important, not urgent. We go to church together – and that's where I look at building that bond of family and faith.

Relooking at my finances, I have reaffirmed that insurance coverage is also vital as I reach another new decade of my life and think of the road ahead.

What are my contributions to society, towards causes I believe in given the platform I have? How can I give back – and how do I want to be remembered? How am I investing in my friendships? I make it a point to meet friends twice a week – and although my friends are varied in personalities, we share similar values.

There are causes I support from working with World Vision and Dignity for Children. For the latter, I strongly believe every child needs access to education. It's a basic human right to level the playing field – and this is the environment I want to create for others (which influences my own environment as well).

How about my love life? Well, I firstly spent a lot of time practicing self-love and self-care – whether it's the external stuff like massages and manicures, or the internal stuff like getting enough sleep and reminding myself that I am enough and loved. I need to complete myself, not someone else.

Tenacious, Vivacious, & Precious

As you can see, everything is important but urgent. You cannot pour from an empty cup. Why am I sharing with you all of this – and what does it have to do with audacity?

In my books, **everything has to do with audacity**. We are not one-dimensional people – and I don't want to be known for only one aspect of my life while sucking in the other areas.

We are multi-dimensional people. Getting to the root of what holds you back – be it self-sabotage or procrastination – we have the tools to get us on track. When we "lack" in other areas of life, we are not playing to the fullness of our audaciousness. What I've shared is not really rocket science; it really is a case of knowing your why.

You know you're precious, tenacious, and vivacious – and that's being audacious.

Birds of Audacious Feathers Flock Together

by Norlida Azmi

Moving forward here, we are going to look at being the kind of audacious which stems from a good place – where the manifestations are of being "bold" and "courageous". The other spectrum – the negative side of audacity – that I referred to in the first chapter is for another time. (Or maybe even another book.)

So: being audacious – is it nature or nurture? To me, it's an evolution, depending on which stage of life you are at, and the experiences that may trigger or accelerate how audacious you want to be (and can be).

Begin with self-reflection and introspection

These days, you hear the younger generation talking and asking about "Purpose" – and they are not wrong. As you reflect about what you want to do and achieve in life, I believe we all want to be great, and to do great things.

"You have to believe in yourself.
You need to have the audacity to be great."

– Rosie Perez

Just saying.

Taking bold actions – especially those that challenge the status quo or areas of comfort – could result in people reacting violently towards you. Criticisms and negative labelling may happen – and no matter how tough you are, it could hurt. Will you be able to steel yourself, and remain focused and committed towards your acts of audacity?

When I have been forced to be in such positions, I allow myself to feel the initial reactions of hurt or anger – because I believe that suppressing emotions, especially negative ones, will adversely impact our overall well-being (if not immediately, definitely later). The trick is **not to wallow in it** – and to refresh your mind and heart with the purpose of your bold actions. This self-talk is to increase the conviction of your beliefs, and to reaffirm that the journey of you achieving greatness is worth it. **Be guided by your purpose.**

If you're blessed to have a really good friend – and that can be in the form of spouse, partner, or a non-related party – s/he/they can help you unpack yourself objectively as you define your purpose. A sounding board can help stretch your mind and nullify your self-doubt – but at the end of it all, you are the one who must decide.

Some of the women I mentor or coach who are moving up the leadership ladder have asked how to take bold measures and to have their voices heard – to transform their careers with new and daring decisions. Whilst talking about building confidence, we also address their appetite for risks. You must understand that by being more daring, you are opening yourself to taking more risks. This is where I apply my prior experience as a risk manager – in that risk is not so much about not doing what you want to do, but understanding what are the mitigating factors and evaluating between what you could lose versus what you might gain.

This reflection at times reveals that we have created those barriers ourselves. Push down those doors that have been in your way; burst into new experiences driven by bold and audacious decisions that will empower you. I can already hear some people saying: "This is already too much analysis" – to which I say: "Just do it!" My comeback is that some people need a little more guidance to unlock their potential and capability to be audacious.

The extent of how audacious you want to be may change over time; **do not be pressured to be who you are not**. It will not be sustainable.

How far are you willing to go? How high do you want to climb? How audacious do you want to be?

Only you can answer those questions.

Keep your validation circle tight with you at the core

Almost everybody has an opinion about everything – and if you care about all their opinions and/or try to please them all, it would be very crippling to you. Our upbringing and societal expectations have shaped many of our pre-dispositions about pleasing other people – but I believe you can define the limits. **Or rather, you must**.

We must not accord too much importance to public opinion. Don't worry too much what others will think of you. Don't overthink: "Will I say the wrong thing? Will I look stupid? Will they think I am crazy?" Mind you, this is not a license to be callous – for you should not wantonly hurt someone – but public opinion should not deter you from doing what you want to do.

Put yourself at the centre and ask yourself: is this what you want, and will you *always* stand by it? Is it aligned to your personal values? That is all that really matters. For me, there is a small circle whose opinions matter – and this may vary according to topics and issues – because they matter. On the flip side, you may be one of those that have no inner circle – or you truly don't care what anyone thinks. If so, so be it: that itself is an audacious position, and you should live by the consequences. For me, this is quite challenging; we are increasingly becoming part of many ecosystems – and to have that impact, I value a small circle for thoughts and feedback.

Organisational culture has increasingly been a space that corporates want to shape, such that the business and employees' goals are met. Often enough in my role, I have to implement "disruptive" or "triggering" programmes that impact people's behaviour. With this, I am confronted with enough cynicism – but my validation circle is comprised of the people who are aligned to the objective, and of my boss who has my back. Everybody else will have an opinion; **I have mine.** I stay focused to deliver what I believe is good – and right.

In my personal life, the validation circle is very small: my immediate family, and my good friends. That's it. Everybody else will have an opinion; I have mine.

Surround yourself with audacious people

Like-minded people tend to gravitate together and cheer you on, as you take on audacious goals. They are also ignited by the desires to be great – and you will be inspired by their energy and their audacity, as they will by yours. In the journey to be great, there will be times when you trip – and this support group of colleagues, friends, or family who understand what you want to be will always be on your side, picking you up and encouraging you because they can empathise with what you want to achieve.

Sometimes, you find inspiration in a group or community that you never thought would inspire you to be audacious. For the most part, I have been fortunate that in the various mentoring or coaching circles that I have been in, the other party has always sparked off in me the need to be better. In one of these instances, the mentee was a young talent who was involved in one of these borderless NGOs – and the way she went about to help people in the outreach engineering projects just blew my mind, inspiring me to find a way to be great in the sustainability space. (In practical terms, not this greenwashing nonsense.)

In the bank that was the most aggressive multinational organisation that I worked at early in my career, most of my then colleagues were high achievers. Remember the

"Second place" mantra I mentioned in the last chapter? This was the place. In a pace that was most times manic, your audacity was not only the goals themselves – but how fast you wanted to achieve them. Some people knock this type of corporate life, but I enjoyed it then. You can imagine the adrenaline rush I experienced then – and I can honestly say it has influenced me tremendously to this day. Today, if I meet them again, I see how far their audacity and boldness have taken them – so, I am grateful to have been in that ecosystem.

I bounce off the energy I get from the people around me – and as such, I stay away from people that sap my enthusiasm for life. **Naysayers will hold you back from being great.**

Spread your wings and fly, at higher altitudes and unknown destinations. Repeat.

> *"We must dare, and dare again, and go on daring."*
> *– Georges Jacques Danton*

I love this quote!

How often do you challenge yourself, and push your mind to think of the unthinkable – to do something that lies outside your comfort zone? At times, we avoid this, because we feel that we don't have the right skill sets; or you have not perfected the concept; or you have never ever done it before. You know what? **Push yourself not by one step, but ten steps!** And keep doing it over and over again – for the same audacious goal, or even another in order to build that audacious muscle.

I enjoyed reading how Sir Richard Branson personifies audacity, along with his advice about starting big, going all in, and never fearing failure. From my viewpoint, it speaks to the first point of believing in ourselves, and building that self-confidence. From there, we channel our passion and conviction in the bold steps that we want to take – and to do it whole-heartedly.

Sir Richard says that "half-heartedly" is the opposite of audacity. It's like dreaming big, and doing bigger – which can be scary. This folds into a third point: for years, in the societies we grew up in, failure was seen as a very negative outcome. It is only in recent years that the mantra of "fail fast, and learn fast" has been propagated – where people finally say that it's okay to fall flat on our face and fail to encourage us to experiment, to be audacious, and to keep going.

In part, our fear to move to an area of discomfort could stem from the difference between being prepared and being ready. Being prepared puts us in the position of undertaking all the physical and mental preparatory steps before taking that big leap – a situation where we would have assessed a higher chance of success. Meanwhile, being ready plays more to the complex state of emotional preparedness, and is generally less under our control than mere logistical steps.

To be audacious, we first have to accept that you won't always be prepared: we need to just do it. Success may not be your first milestone – but you will definitely grow. During this undertaking, you begin to realise that the safety net has been taken away – and the fear will ebb as you build the courage to fly. **Because you dared**.

I have some good friends at work – but even they sometimes shake their heads at me. I remember one time when two of my most capable colleagues came into the room, closed the door and said: "Boss, we have come to do a group intervention." In essence, it was to temper an ambitious programme that I wanted to mobilise. They came from a position of care – but we forged ahead with the original plan, because we needed to take bold actions in order to make that difference.

We remain friends, and they still call me a crazy boss – but they do acknowledge the value and success. Sometimes, we fly alone at the start, and bring others along the way. Perhaps that can inspire them to be as audacious.

As the world gets more connected, we are exposed to more role models of audacity, and in different spaces. We delve into their roots, and follow their life journeys to get inspiration. However, at the end of it all, we all define HOW we want to be audacious: the impact and legacy that we want to be known for as a result of our own choice.

Audacious is Personal.

Sita's Triumphant Audacity

by Sharma Kumari

The Backstory

When she was 16, Sita married into a small family. There was her husband, her father-in-law, and a brother-in-law. The two brothers had lost their mother at a young age, and were brought up primarily by their father.

A widower at a very young age, Sita's father-in-law had never remarried despite the pressure to do so way back then. His pushback stemmed from the unsavory tales he had heard about stepmothers – and there was no way he wanted to subject his boys to any avoidable misfortune.

Amidst this, we had the beautiful, docile, demure Sita stepping into this small all-male world some years later.

An interesting custom observed in Sita's community then was that as a mark of respect, a daughter-in-law should not have any direct conversation with her father-in-law. In addition to this, the daughter-in-law was also required to cover her head with a long shawl (*dupatta*) as a mark of respect towards elders. Should Sita ever need to communicate with her father-in-law, it would have to be indirectly, either through her husband or any other family member.

Imagine being in the same household, carrying out all domestic chores and duties, breathing the same air – and never being able to freely ask or say anything to the head of the family. However, as it was an accepted norm then, it appeared to work well.

This custom played out for almost 30 years – by which time, there were seven children in the family. They had an excellent bond with their grandfather, who proved to be the doting, loving, and pampering grandparent that every child deserves. The children became a communication bridge between their mother and their grandfather.

Sita's husband was caught-up mostly with managing the sundry shop business that his father had started years ago. This included juggling the ups and downs of a once-flourishing business, looking into feeding a household of ten, as well as educating each of the seven children. All this with a moderate income – which, through his diligence and hard work, grew steadily over the years.

Gradually, the aging process caught up with Sita's father-in-law. His conversations would sometimes suggest that he was in a different location or period of his life, as reflected by the various narratives from the past. He could forget basic things like having eaten and wanting his meal served (again). In the absence of anyone else around, Sita was confused how she could indicate to him that he had eaten; after all, it wasn't as if she **had** forgotten to serve him. Her husband and she decided it was easier to give him another serving – which he hardly touched – rather than try to convince him that he had eaten. This could involve serving the same meal up to three times a day!

As the children grew up and left home, her father-in-law's dependent care fell mainly on Sita. She carried this out with total dedication and care. However, this was increasingly difficult, as her father-in-law became more withdrawn and needing more assistance. It was frustrating for Sita to be unable to impart simple instructions like: "Move to the side."; "Lift yourself."; "Have your food now."; and other routine requests.

Sita realised that to bring the 30-year tradition of no direct communication to an end, she had to enlist support at various levels. Sita's first bold step was to share her plight with her mother, who was the bastion of this age-old tradition. Imagine her mother's consternation, as she too had never spoken with Sita's father-in-law. Although she understood her daughter's plight, she was concerned with "what people would say".

The next discussion Sita had was with her husband, who was more aware of the situation. She emphasised the need for direct communication with his father – and after some balancing of counter-discussion points, it was agreed that it was the best way forward.

Sita's audacity broke a three-decade-old tradition and facilitated her first ever direct communication with her father-in-law. As a result, although the children found it strange to see their mother speaking directly with their grandfather, it meant that she was better able to manage him.

My Mother Sita

Sita is my mother. Born in 1930, she has lived in a time where formal education – and specifically, tertiary education – wasn't a natural progression for most girls.

She was informally educated in her vernacular for a short period by a community priest in the village. I recall how the term "uneducated" was applied back then to those not formally educated to converse in English or – to some extent – the national language. I used to cringe when several teachers at school referred to some of our mothers as "uneducated".

Yet, the hand that rocks the cradle rules the world. As I look back at all that I have seen, heard, or known about her life, I cannot help but admire the grace with which my mother continues to live through her 92nd year. It dawns upon me that audacity has been central to who she is today, and to what she wanted each of her seven children to be.

In his 2019 blog entry entitled *Achieving The Audacious*, business strategist Richard Shrapnel said: "Audacious is not reckless, careless, negligent, or prideful. It is thoughtful, committed, and relentless. It is certainly purposeful with clear outcomes sought."

This exactly describes my ever-so-patient mother Sita. She was thoughtful, not prideful; committed, not negligent; relentless, not careless.

In addition to it all, what she did have was a vision.

The Audacity Continuum Matrix that we were introduced to in the previous chapter is aligned to what Shrapnel expressed: For one to be thoughtful, committed, and relentless, there is a need for an emotional connection with our beliefs before we are driven to act with conviction.

This is How We Do It

1. Life may have dealt you a bad hand. Be audaciously in control.

My mother could have begrudged the lack of opportunity for a formal education. She could have chosen to be confined to the one and only language she then knew how to read: the Punjabi script (*Gurmukhī*). Instead, she redirected her attention to the daily English language newspaper *The Straits Times* – and later, the *New Straits Times* – delivered at our doorstep. Without knowing the spelling of a single word in English, she drew upon the syntax in *Gurmukhī* that she was familiar with to know that words are formed by letters, that each one has its own peculiar sound: and when strung together, they become distinguishing words.

At that point of time, there was no television in the house. She must have paid attention to the chatter of her children, as they dominantly spoke English amongst themselves. She would then introduce some English phrases into her vocabulary. One of them was: "What don't know?!?" when we tried to be dismissive in our answers. She caught us at our game!

My mother would also hold up the broadsheet newspaper and slowly read by connecting the syllables. She not only challenged herself at the risk of being laughed at, but also allowed her children to correct her.

That picture is still vivid in my mind.

My father, too, was impressed by her perseverance, and often admired her ability to take to languages with ease. He was amazed at how she could watch TV serials in any language and accurately pick up the nuances and storyline. She had over the years learnt to communicate with friends and neighbours in Bahasa Malaysia, Cantonese, Tamil, English, and – of course – her native Punjabi and Hindi languages. This very moment as I am writing this, she is watching a Turkish serial – undubbed. Just ask her the story!

2. Rome was not built in one day. Be audaciously relentless.

Taking the path of least resistance will work in situations where it is best to avoid being unnecessarily confrontational. However, when we have a dream, a vision, or a belief, it will bear fruit only if we relentlessly pursue it by working around obstacles.

My parents were highly committed and focused on educating their children. However, we were not coerced or bribed to do so; we weren't even scolded for poor grades.

Instead, my father would sign our report cards without looking at our grades. My favorite strategy was to get his signature when he was engrossed in his favorite pastime: playing chess.

Should my mother or eldest sibling alert him to this, his usual response was: "Someone has to sweep the roads. Study if you want to." My father was not putting anyone nor any vocation down; he was merely being realistic about effort and outcome.

For me, though, that hit home hard.

My father's relentless reverse psychology in not pushing us to study nor setting any benchmark for grades made us chart our own course. It instilled ownership and accountability in us. Looking back at my parents, they were relentless with themselves too. For years, they denied themselves the "luxury" of a TV set – until we were all in secondary and tertiary education. (To digress, what a grand entry though, as the TV came in conjunction with World Cup 1974. The Beckenbauer-Cryuff face-off then, with the Messi-Mbappe "GOAT" race to the finish now.)

The eldest amongst us is my sister. She finished her A-Levels, which was equivalent to Form 6 in the early 1970s. She was keen to go to university. However, because it meant adding a financial burden, it was decided that perhaps getting her married would be the better option. My sister was determined to study, and refused to give in. She appealed to my plucky grandfather and my mother for moral support.

My sister got her wish as she always did. This then paved the way for all the others, especially us girls in the family, to have tertiary education. My mother has been steadfast about this. Until today, she encourages her grandchildren to continue studying up to post-graduate level as she emphasizes that nothing empowers and liberates like education.

3. Find your true north. Be audaciously authentic.

Authenticity propels us forward. It is aligned with our internal compass.

My mother was from a generation that was expected to toe the line, to accept the role of playing second fiddle, to upkeep traditions unquestioningly. Putting aside the period or geo-location of where we are – should we even accept that we are meant to be externally defined?

Even as we conform to certain practices and societal expectations of us, I dare say, the inner voice will cry out to remind us what truly defines us. It will question us on our choices if they are not aligned with our value system. How often have we shut out that voice – only for it to come back again at some point?

I consider it necessary to tune in and listen to this inner voice of ours. This is us – our authentic true north. It is a combination of **what we value most** and **what we know to be our purpose**. When our actions are aligned with our true north, we are at ease and feel light – just like we are being propelled forward.

Similarly, my mother was in a quandary: should she upkeep the old tradition of not speaking with her father-in-law – and as a result, deny him the care and attention that he needed? Or should she listen to her inner voice to communicate and be with him in this helpless state?

No one could answer that question for her – not anyone from within the family, nor from the larger society. It had to come from her – and it did.

Audacity is allowing your authenticity to shine through so that you become the best version of yourself. My mother was driven by her naturally empathetic and caring self – that had always been her true north. She was thankful to be able to communicate directly with her father-in-law. On his better days, he would cooperate, respond, and even have short conversations with her (and the rest of us). I could sense my mother's relief at having pushed the envelope and fighting off the (dare I say it? Senseless!) societal norms.

She did not care about her own massive weight loss in the process. My grandfather's physical mobility decreased with age. My mother did everything, from giving him a bed bath daily, to feeding him, and cleaning after him. He was almost like a baby in her arms.

To her credit, in the two years or so that he was in this condition, my grandfather never developed a single bed sore – which, according to doctors, was a remarkable achievement.

The height of our pain was when he passed away – and even then, he was cradled in my father's arms and with my mother holding on to him. We lost a grandfather who was a great friend. My father had lost his dear dad, the bedrock of his existence. But my mother, she cried just as if she had lost a beloved baby.

It was such a poignant moment – but one with no regrets, especially on the part of my mother.

That is how my mother did Audacity.

By being in control. Relentless. And authentic.

The Road to Growth is Paved with Audacious Weirding

by Syireen Rose

What is normal? How do we normalise? When did the new normal kick in? If the new is normal, then was the old abnormal? How do we know if we are normal or otherwise? What is the benchmark for normal?

My answer: I don't know.

But normally, when a young child is asked: "When you grow up, what would you like to be?", the child is expected to answer: "Doctor"; "Lawyer"; "Accountant". And then, the teacher looked at me – and I quipped gleefully: "Happy". It sounded quite logical to me – until my teacher said: "Happy will not make you rich". I promptly asked her: "What is rich?" – and she stared at me like I was a Gremlin snarling back at her at midnight.

My unorthodox answer didn't go down very well in school, where children are expected to be excited and grow up to work for money – and the teacher's response definitely didn't quite fit in my head that was already filled with Enid Blyton and the Faraway Tree; because in my world of literature and books I enjoyed magical trees that could take me anywhere and everywhere; and wizards and witches who could pull off mumbo jumbos, and create a world filled with whatever I wanted!

Who needs "rich" when I can be "happy", right?!?

Yeah, I was a weird kid…

In kindergarten, while girls would giggle themselves silly while playing with Barbies, I'd be out the back with the boys playing with sand in a box, getting super dirty, and thinking it was funny – until mom said it wasn't… Girls are dressed in pink, and behave prim and properly – whereas I was just… well, NOT! Then the kids would run off and play catch in the sun; get into groups, and play hopscotch; or hop around with skipping ropes, while I decided to stay in and colour my heart out – because sharpening colour pencils produced fun stuff that I could stick to papers, which looked like a rainbow of flowers. I'd make a mess though, so the teachers frowned – and mom got called in. Then, I'd listen to other little girls like me talk about their cute cartoon crushes like He-Man or Prince Charming – while I fell in love with Optimus Prime, the lead Autobot who could just transform into a trailer truck that I could "roll out" in!

What can I say? To a certain extent, I was an oddball.

As I grew up and being rich evolved into an important topic of conversations, marrying the right guy became a priority. Given that little girls were fed with Disney's damsels-in-distress needing-to-be-saved storylines, being rich equated to marrying a prince who lived in a castle and rode on a white horse. So, having the right boyfriend was a good start.

I thought so too – until I found out that rich boys can't dance, are not funny, and they talked about their daddy's car like it belonged to them, whereas the reality was that they could not even afford their own underwear (an overgeneralisation, of course). I felt that whole idea was troublesome – so, I befriended a boy who would draw me flowers: he made me very happy. We never dated, because that was just so "Ewwwwww, disgusting!", so I never had a boyfriend throughout high school – and that, by an all-girl's school's standards, was weird.

High school also meant getting loads of "A"s – and I was under a lot of pressure to perform, because I was sent to a prestigious all-girl's school. Unfortunately, every year the record would show a combined 3.5 months of absenteeism, and an unsurmountable amount of homework that I never submitted. I consistently performed poorly at every exam, except for English and History. I was doomed to be an underperformer because I diligently failed.

Yet, I told my mother that I didn't need anything except for a good command of the language and an understanding of life to be a writer. I wanted to travel the world and write about my experiences on it – just like the history books I read. She said, bless her soul: "Writing won't make you rich…" Since I didn't have much of a choice, I decided to strive ONLY for national exams – and scored my "A"s, and got my scholarship. My mother sent me out to apply for Accountancy; I applied for a degree in Journalism – and graduated as a writer instead.

What can I say? Writing makes me ridiculously happy – even when I was told I could not make a living out of it. Gosh: the weirdo in me simply outdid herself!

I don't quite remember the whirlwind of college life – but I remembered being a loner. I walked alone; I lived alone; I studied alone. I vividly remember having friends – but none that were deep nor lasting for me to revisit and reminisce about college with a group of mates. I remembered having fun that made me reluctant to go home, but I can't pinpoint the experiences.

I don't think I have pictures either, because I never bothered. It was four years of nullness in terms of relationships. But I remembered the beauty of autumn; watching this beautiful girl with blue hair walk pass my school like clockwork; the solace of walking home from the library at night; sleeping amidst lit candles; and that big tree out of my window that truly kept me company.

Looking back, I lived my life independently and went against every norm – so much so that the Malaysian Student Representative called me regularly to check on my sanity, because he received multiple reports from Malaysian students about me being *sesat* ("astray"). He said that I needed spiritual help, and that I needed the right company to keep me to my roots – so I went to the animal shelter, and adopted a Maine Coon. I was told that cats ward off evil, which I felt was very spiritual – and I called him Bud.

Upon graduation, my collegemates targeted the main media houses and I followed them to queue in line for the interviews: TV3 *lah*; the *New Straits Times lah*; *The Star lah*. Eventually, I thought about it – and felt that all these agencies were so big lah that I decided to apply for a startup in an incubation centre instead. Everyone I knew got paid between RM1,800 to RM2,200 – but I accepted a job that paid me RM1,600 and that started at 7am and ended way into the night (because my boss started his day at 2pm, and ran his meetings at 7pm).

It wasn't the best of experiences. I had several jobs after that – and it simply didn't work. My jobs exposed me to patriarchy, sexism, and bullying at every turn of my working day. It was the worst few years of my life – but it showed me what I **didn't** need in my life. Finally, five years into employment, I quit without any backup plan nor future income – and became the second member of my family to embark on the unfamiliar path of entrepreneurism. With no references or like-minded peers in sight, I started my business in editorial services because writing makes me happy.

My outfit Peaches 'N Pen started off as a sole proprietorship – and five years in, it became a partnership. Throughout the process, I had more misses than hits. With no mentor nor guru, nor any understanding of a business model, my entire setup was focused on how much money I can make, and how long I can stretch the dollar.

Little did I know that freelancing is not a business – and that the outfit was just a shell to ensure that there was a bank account for clients to make payment. I once got seriously insulted in a session, where a mature business lady told me that I didn't have a business because I was a freelancer. I told her she was wrong; how could I be a freelancer when I had registered an entity where the income goes to the "business"?

It was a hard slap in the face – and my ego was bruised. I refused to accept the truth. I went through it for a few more years, bulldozing my way, and never truly figuring out what I needed – but proudly claiming myself as a business owner. The lifestyle fit me, until my family grew from two to five in a span of six years.

I had to return to employment for a steady income, though I kept Peaches 'N Pen on the side because I just love to write. I stayed employed for four years – and I went against every norm of the organisation. I was called many things in the process: I was a "loose cannon"; I was "reckless"; I was "immature"; and much more – because of my choice of discipline and presentation.

I stood my ground, because I believed in delivering quality, and not just making promises that I couldn't keep. I kept standards high – which got my colleagues upset, and they found every way possible to make my approach wrong. I had a seriously tough time – and my increment plus bonus reflected the "punishment" the management imposed on me.

I did it anyway, because my work produced results – but it finally came down to a threat: whereby they would hold my job advancement and privileges against me if I did not change. I was to be demoted – even though I was the only one qualified for the job. However, the beauty of a bully's mindset is that it is predictable; they thought that by threatening me, I would cave in and change my ways.

So, I quit!

They were shocked, and told me to reconsider – but my decision made me immensely happy. This despite the fact that by then, I ended up very broke – with another baby on the way.

Indeed, throughout my entire life, my decision-making patterns have been the opposite of what is commonly and popularly done. Each decision would raise eyebrows; most decisions created discomfort amongst peers. And yet, at junctions, I would trudge the path most uncommonly walked upon – a perfect poster for motivation, but not if you expected to earn a living. One of my good friends called me "weird" – and I thought that was befitting, because there simply was no benchmark to measure me against. No one could handle me, and for a while, I thought something was wrong – until I stared at myself in the mirror, and only saw a perfectly normal human being staring back at me.

Having written only partially of how I approached life, most would have found this individual (me) exceptionally exasperating and difficult. Yet, at the same time, the very society which negated my ways would cheer, applaud, and honour strong women portrayed in movies: – Erin Brockovich (played by Julia Roberts); Miranda Priestly (played by Meryl Streep in *The Devil Wears Prada*); G.I. Jane (played by Demi Moore); and Maleficent (played by Angelina Jolie) – these women took a stand for their beliefs. Just as I do. These women would not negotiate their rights nor their pride, nor would they devalue themselves to fit in. Just as I would not do. These women were shunned and shoved by society, and labeled as the worst – but they rose up strong and won their battles. Just as I did.

The audacity of strong-minded individuals going against the grain and doing what is right is commonly viewed negatively – until the strength and faith in truth withstands all odds, and stands triumphant by being exactly who they really are. Like these women, I cannot be anyone else but me – and in all audacity, I only wanted to be happy, leading me to stop doing what made me miserable.

I never intended to make things harder than it should be, nor did I purposely lay out a plan to aggravate situations with critical discourse – because I insist on clarity. The fact is, I fought hard to be happy – and for that, I am AUDACIOUSLY WEIRD in all my undertakings and decisions.

I am, alas, an audaciously happy gal. If I'm audacious as anything else, I leave it to you to define...

CHAPTER 3
Being Audacious Pays

Audaciously Deservable

by Syireen Rose

I am a firm believer that everything is by design – and until we understand this fact of life, the Master of the Universe will consistently, persistently, and audaciously help all forms of sh*t to hit the fan until we get the message; because if you don't already know, the Universe is constantly conspiring in our favour. It is unfortunate that we deny favours so fervently that favours need to detour and seek different avenues – in forms of challenges, losses, grievances, and everything else that life would throw us – so that we would be driven to rise at every occasion so that the favours can finally arrive to its rightful owner: YOU and ME!

It boils down to our levels of "deservability". Do you believe that you deserve it? What do you want?

I grew up never once thinking of being a millionaire/billionaire/gazillionaire. Not that I didn't dream of a big house – but because I was raised in one, I had no need for another. I did, however, entertain the thought of a mansion on top of a hill overlooking the sea. I wanted horses to ride across the fields, and I wanted a boat that I could get on from the dock that lay somewhere alongside the waterfront where my house would be built. I would see a trail that takes me into the forests behind my home, so I could stand on a hilltop and watch the boats go by.

In my youth, my future had it all; in my mind, my future self had it all. It's just that I never designed my dream to be wrapped up in dollars and cents – so, I didn't need to be a millionaire to access it. Because of that mindset, I didn't have a need for a lot of money.

However, I worked hard for happiness – and that included wealth creation for both myself, and for the people I love.

I measured all my success against being happy. I felt happy thinking of a big house on a hill overlooking the sea – so I aimed to own it. I felt happy dreaming about my horse, my boat, my sea, as I admittedly described rather vividly above. I felt happy imagining it all – so I aimed at owning it. Money was not my benchmark; I wanted to grow up and be happy.

My benchmark of wealth answers the questions: "Are you happy?" and "What do you need to be happy?"

Ironically, I grew up and landed onto the path of entrepreneurship – where becoming a millionaire is the mantra for existence. Apparently, in entrepreneurship – or at least, to the one that I was exposed to – equates life success and happiness to being rich! Every programme I'd enter would begin by asking the golden question: "How many of you would like to be a millionaire?" – and all hands would rise in unison. Being part of the herd, my hands were often part of that sea of enthusiastic millionaire wannabe. Yet once I left these pumped up and energised rooms, my head goes right into my "happy cloud" – where it stays until I attend another entrepreneurial programme that conditions and conditions and conditions the pool of millionaire wannabes that being rich is the only goal – and that anything else is failure.

It's not rocket science that I was a miserable wreck for not being "rich". Sure, I would want the nice handbag, because I wanted to fit in but not because I liked it. It was just what I had been conditioned to believe was that rich and successful people MUST have branded items. I would scour fashion magazines to keep on top of what's trending – so that I could be dressed to fit the crowd, and stand out with the latest designs. I needed a nice car; I needed the latest handphone; I wanted what the other guy and gal had that screams: "SUCCESS!!!"

I felt like a schizophrenic imposter, believing that what I saw was what was right – and yet not really feeling it. In reflection, I was a psychological mess.

I could never get the right clients, nor the right balance sheet. I kept on inviting the wrong partners – who'd either over-leverage me, take advantage of me, or literally run off with the business that I had built, lock, stock, and barrel. I was told I had a poor relationship with money – that I didn't have a BIG DREAM, and that I had no urgency to reach for the stars. I was also told that I lived in a bubble with a very small financial container – so theoretically, I can never enlarge it to fill it fully.

So, I was not going to be rich any time soon – and yet, when observing my environment, I found myself no less happy (nor sadder) than the millionaires and billionaires that I'd met.

Looking back, I had lived three decades of being neither here nor there, because I was fed the idea of what I deserved – and I was convinced to believe in a reality that was outside of my actual one. I kept on thinking that I was such a failure for not hitting my million, my fancy car, my luxurious apartment, my designer outfits – year in and year out.

Yet, upon reflection, I already knew since childhood what "deserving" looked like – but I was disillusioned by a system driven by hedonism and economic triumphs that dubbed my dream of happiness as success to be mere child's play. It was indeed a chaotic 30 years of soul searching; of high and lows; massive confusion; self-esteem battering that came simply from being misaligned. While trying to fit in, I lost me – and thus never got what I truly deserve.

Paddling back to that point in time where I dreamt of a life rooted in happiness, the girl who was audaciously designing her dream life as she deemed fit was simply seeking to fulfil a different need – and that was the need for mindfulness and emotional stability.

I come from a broken home. I was raised by a single mother who barely made ends meet on her own, so I was raised by a home full of relatives. I really don't have fuzzy warm stories to tell – and that should be enough for readers to gauge why I aim for happiness. I dreamt of mindfulness, kindness, a sense of belonging, laughter, relationships: a home that would grant me emotional stability. My mansion, as I dreamt it, is warm with love, laughter, and family presence. My world is vast and free as the ocean, and trails up hilltops that are all enveloped in love.

This is wealth to me – and I truly and audaciously deserve it.

I worked hard at building my legacy of wealth – and I guard my heart jealously.

I just didn't realise how my subconscious kept nudging me towards my true goal. The unconscious mind hears well – and I must say, I had worked audaciously against all entrepreneurial mantras. I broke every rule about the notion of wealth – and I am still breaking it audaciously well.

This is who I am today, against all odds.

I am An Audaciously Deserving Wife

I was an only child. My mother raised me on her own – and it was always just the two of us. It was normal to just have a mom until I went to school – and I watched others have a set of parents whereas mine was a "2-in-1". I watched a lot of TV – and I observed other people's family, which I assumed were complete. I also observed my uncle, whose family was my benchmark.

Although I did not know it then, I had designed my life based on my checklist of conditions for satisfaction – and it started with the man I would marry.

My uncle put his wife on the highest pedestal. He cooked and cleaned, and raised his boys. They went on holidays, and he was always very funny. He had a nice quaint home, a nice car, and was always kind. I never heard him raise his voice. So, yeah: my man was going to be a family man who would put me on the highest of pedestals – because I am a deserving Queen.

Of course!

Then I watched Snow White, and I didn't like that queen at all. So, I designed a nicer queen for myself, and studied what makes a good wife. I had my checklist for myself too – because if I were deserving of a King, then I had to be an equal match.

Still, when I met him, I set my standards high. I told him that I don't cook, I don't clean, and that I am always chauffeured. He said: "OK." – and he married me. We spent a decade struggling to make ends meet, because we were young and didn't know what we were doing. We had three boys in those 10 years – and in that time, I did cook, and I did clean, and I drove myself to and from my destination because I could. (Until recently, that is.)

As I write this, we had both created a pretty decent life for ourselves; we've crossed two decades of marital life, with three boys and one girl now. Our life is much more settled – and now I don't cook, I don't clean, and I am chauffeured, because that was how I designed my deserving life. I am held on the highest pedestal because I paid my dues. I am queen of the house – and everything I say goes, unless the King says otherwise (which is almost never).

Clearly, I got what I wanted.

The point is: the little girl had a plan, but life throws curveballs. Nothing comes without sacrifices – but because I had a dream of an audaciously mindful and happy life, I kept focus on my definition of wealth.

I am now an audaciously deserving happy wife!

I am An Audaciously Deserving Mother

I was called many names: Momster! Momzilla! Mother of Dragons! You name it, I was labelled it. Those were labels "gifted" to me by many "by-the-books" mummies who adopted many Western ways of upbringing. I went against every ounce of the grain that fit the "perfect modern mom".

Society thought I was unforgivingly delinquent – because I raised my kids so differently.

The baby books tell mothers to keep to a schedule. Meanwhile, I decided that time is relative, and that I would feed the kids when they're hungry. They sleep whenever they get sleepy – and they consume however much they need when they felt hungry. So, there was no feeding every 2-4 hours; there was no nap time; no rush-rush-rush to put kids to sleep. My kids were everywhere, and doing everything – it's called experiencing life!

The rule of thumb, according to "experts", was to feed the kids solids and get them on a routine after six months. My kids were on breast milk and supplementary milk for 24 months. They ate whatever and whenever – and only if they wanted to. I never packed food, because I whipped "food" out of my shirt, and they eat off of my plate, should they find my plate of food interesting; otherwise, I just let them suckle and suckle.

And no, I was not a soccer mom, nor did I spoil them silly. I was not their driver; I was not their nanny; I was not their cook nor their cleaner. I didn't hustle and bustle around their calendar. Everybody either picks up after themselves, or the home is left as it is.

I have never felt the need for shame for the shipwreck that I called home.

I was a working mom and I had kids – and I had to go to work and participate in the creation of our family's economics. I audited my time; I audited my money; and I audited my space 24/7. My time was divided in quarters: to manage the home, the business, the extra-curricular activities, and my personal health. I played tag team with hubby and in-laws to drop the kids off to school and tuition – and we picked them up after school in turns. I carted them everywhere I went when I could – and left them at my in-laws when I couldn't. I hated leaving my babies – but I had a job to do.

I refuse to be judged for doing the best that I could with the resources and knowledge I had back then.

I raised them with the utmost regimented life. No TV unless granted; no junk food, and no cordials; no sweets, and no coloured foods; no fizzy drinks, and no fast food. Do as you are told, or you get a time out! Go where I go – and stay where I tell you to stay.

In hindsight, I sounded like a nightmare and I probably was – making decisions out of necessity.

And yet, I have so many beautiful photos of memorable moments. I cannot fathom how I managed – but every quarter of the year, we would have quality time at Kuantan or Port Dickson, which we could afford. Sometimes, we had extra and we'd go further – to Pulau Kapas, or higher up to Genting Highlands. We got lucky on several occasions due to our network – and my boys got to see Disney on Ice, and tickets to Riding Competitions – and later in life, they enjoyed hot air balloons.

I also managed personalised fables that they remember till today as bedtime lullabies. I held them all the time, kissed them, snuggled with them, went crazy silly, and laughed madly – because I was and still am genuinely madly in love with my munchkins, and I made sure they knew it. In between the madness, the screaming, the unbecoming behaviours of losing my temper and my mind – somehow, they always knew how precious they are to me, and they always forgave me.

Then our lives took a turn – and we could take our children to Australia and Hong Kong! Life got so much better – and Ummi got more time to let loose. I spent more and more quality time with them.

Today, my sons would insist that they drive me to and from locations when they can. My children work the house, cook, and clean, and serve my every whim. They buy my favourite food and snacks. They bend themselves backwards to see me smile. My birthdays are filled with amazing surprises that used to be bought by hubby on their behalf – and now, it's all from their own pocket money and hard-earned change.

I still kiss them silly in public now that they are adults; hug them, and tickle them in broad daylight; I play with them – and most preciously, they will respond back with: "I love you, Ummi." Other mummies who used to frown at me and my unorthodox child-rearing methods now lament how their kids don't listen, don't talk, and refuse to be in their company.

Oh, well…

I once asked my kids: "Did you ever figure out why I was angry and temperamental?" They said: "No." "Are you upset with me for screaming at you?" They said: "No.", and jokingly demonstrated how I look like a hyena when I do. When I asked them: "How come?" They told me, separately: "Because Ummi loves me." – which they follow up with a kiss for me before they cordially walk away.

Every time I second-guessed myself, they will say: "It's okay – we know, you love us, and we understand. Life is hard."

I am indeed blessed and humbled by the gift that He has granted me – and indeed, I accept that I am an audaciously deserving mother, for going against the grain while raising my kids in a way I believed would make them worthy men and women of this world – all while the world expected different of me.

I am An Audaciously Deserving Leader

Many of my updates, articles, and books would share various nuggets of my insights into leadership. The journey had been an uphill battle – and I had always been the most reluctant leader at the helm. I consistently and repeatedly declined every role – and each time I walked away, I get persuaded into shoes that I felt I could not fit.

I learned that lessons must be learned for each of us to grow up – only to be greeted with more lessons. Clearly, life is a series of lessons – and for me, I had to learn my pathway that spelt leadership and entrepreneurship – both were roles I never imagined I would ever undertake.

And so, at every opportunity, I would fight it. And yes! The lessons were harder and harsher because I was not a willing receiver. I was a horrible student – and every "teacher" was just more vicious than the one before. I would crash and burn. Rise from the ashes, only to fall back hard on myself and have sand kicked into my face. I would be stabbed and bludgeoned, rebelled against, and betrayed. I would lose friends, and continuously made very few in between.

In my 20s, my conversations were mocked – and my leaders thought I was a loose cannon. When I was in my 30s, an expatriate told me that I was not worthy of being an adviser to Malaysia's prime university. When I was in my 40s, I was told that my leadership sucked, and that I was where I was purely by association and not through merit.

It was a whirlwind of self-doubt and morale badgering years.

Ironically, although I was never popular, I always remained the favourite choice to lead and make things happen. When push comes to shove, and when no one is willing to eat the dust, my name wins the ballot – yet, all my wins came without accolades. My solutions were taken without acknowledgement. The successes I racked were received without any mention of my part in them. I just had to excel and be excellent – but no one would allow me to own my hard work; that is, until I decided to own my leadership, and stand up in my own light.

I started to take leadership, and refused to sit in anyone's shadow. I stopped being the sidekick and the appendix. I even stopped taking meeting minutes just because I was the girl in the room full of men. The moment I stepped into the limelight, and refused to entertain all the bullies, was when I learned my lessons – and then, there was just no turning back!

Today, at the time of writing, I lead leaders of leaders, and I consult, coach, and facilitate various CEOs – from startups, to SMEs, to major organisations in respective industries.

Not bad for a reluctant leader, eh?

I am now, after three decades of learning, an audaciously deserving leader.

As I will be entering into my Five Series in a couple of years as at the time of writing, I believe that I have become an audaciously deserving, proud, and independent woman. After all that – the crashes, the burnings, the stabbings, the bludgeoning – I have wiped clean every drop of bloody tears, stood tall, and won my battles.

I revisited the girl who dreamed of a mansion on a hill overlooking the sea, with horses running up the trail in my backyard to the hilltop, where I can see all the boats and the vast ocean, with my own boat waiting at the docks for my family and I .

I had never let my dream go.

As I end this piece, in all honesty, I sighed a little and realised that I have not only shared with you my journey for choosing to audaciously live by my rules, and by my design, how I had learned that not all society's expectations must be met – I have also declared what my wealth will look like, which is not benchmarked against monetary success but by my happiness with my family.

It is a choice to believe and to live well. It pays to be audacious.

Hence, I am Audaciously Deserving.

Go that Extra Mile

by Sharma Kumari

Nitpicking

There is quite a divide on whether "audacity" is a negative or positive quality. Either comes with its own perspective – but let's refer this to the favourite age-old arbitrator: the dictionary.

Cambridge Dictionary

- courage or confidence of a kind that **other people find shocking or rude**

- unusually strong and especially **rude confidence in yourself**

Oxford Dictionary

- a willingness to take bold risks

- **rude or disrespectful** behaviour; **impudence**

Merriam Webster Dictionary

- intrepid boldness
- **bold or arrogant disregard** of **normal restraints**

Macmillan Dictionary

- the confidence to say or do what you want, despite difficulties, risks, **or the negative attitudes of other people**

From the above, we get a sense that audacity instills courage in people, equips them with adventurous boldness, supports their willingness to take bold risks, and gives them the confidence to say or do what they want in the face of difficulties. Until this point, it seems that audacity is associated with strength, and generates a positive feeling.

Which is good, right?

The definitions also suggest that when this courage or confidence propels one to question long-held boundaries and norms, then audacity could be viewed negatively – probably by those who feel directly challenged. The audacious could then be regarded as improper, rude, impudent, arrogant, disrespectful, and even shocking.

Let's look at this through the actions of a young and famous personality amidst us.

Greta's Great Grimace

The world's climate is the most critical item in the global agenda, and each of us needs to do our part. With this, I have chosen modern-day youth icon Greta Thunberg, who is popularly hailed as an environmental activist.

From the tender age of eight, she became aware of climate change and its impact on the increasing temperature on the Earth's surface. A video at school on the effects of climate change flashed disturbing images of floods, extreme weather, and starving polar bears, amongst other images. This deeply affected Greta, who was baffled as to how we could even be in this situation.

She became withdrawn and slipped into a depression by the age of 11. For the sake of her happiness, Greta's parents made lifestyle changes to reduce carbon emissions at home by installing solar panels, to stop the consumption of meat, and to give up air travel. When she was diagnosed with Asperger's Syndrome, they could put their daughter's extreme reaction towards climate change and her abnormalities in social interaction into perspective.

Climate change was Greta's topmost preoccupation. At 15, she tweeted: "We kids most often don't do what you tell us to do. We do as you do. And since you grown-ups don't give a damn about my future, I won't either. My name is Greta and I'm in ninth grade. And I am school striking for the climate until election day."

She meant every word. For three weeks leading up to the Swedish election, Greta sat alone outside the Swedish Parliament every school day, holding a sign that read in Swedish: "School Strike for Climate." Amidst the heat waves and wildfires in the country, she boldly insisted for the government to reduce carbon emissions aligned with the Paris Agreement.

Her daily strike morphed into the weekly #FridaysForFuture movement, supported by fellow school peers. It grew into a massive, global youth-led climate strike movement – and Greta was now a role model inspiring millions to act against climate change.

Many of us have seen or heard Greta's bold and impassioned speech when she addressed the United Nation's Climate Action Summit on Monday, Sept 23, 2019. The moderator's question to her was: "What's your message to the world leaders today?"

Greta's opening words were: "My message is that we'll be watching you."

The audience reaction was mixed; amidst the applause, there was laughter that appeared to belittle her. However, nothing deterred Greta's grit. She was already emotionally armed with facts and data, and knew exactly what her message was.

Visibly furious with tears of rage, the young Swedish activist said: "This is all wrong. I shouldn't be up here. I should be back in school on the other side of the ocean. Yet you all come to us young people for hope. **How dare you!** You have stolen my dreams and my childhood with your empty words. And yet I'm one of the lucky ones. People are suffering. People are dying. Entire ecosystems are collapsing. We are in the beginning of a mass extinction, and all you can talk about is money and fairy tales of eternal economic growth. **How dare you!**"

From that point, Greta did not hold back. She proceeded to harangue the audience for daring to continue ignoring more than three decades of scientific evidence, for mouthing empty promises about rectifying the situation, and how their suggested solutions were laughably inadequate – because it is HER generation and future ones who would still have to pay the ultimate price.

To an audience that clearly was showing discomfort at her words, Greta ended her speech with a stern promise: "You are failing us. But the young people are starting to understand your betrayal. The eyes of all future generations are upon you. And if you choose to fail us, I say: **We will never forgive you**. We will not let you get away with this. Right here, right now is where we draw the line. The world is waking up. And change is coming, whether you like it or not."

Decorum in the UN calls for basic diplomatic respect, with language that creates a safe space. The UN chair is empowered to request decorum if delegates are loud or disrespectful. However, there was no call out – because the young lady spoke the truth, the whole truth, and nothing but the truth.

Greta was not called out – not then, and not during the 2021 UN Climate Change Conference (COP26) where she told world leaders that their words sound great but were "...30 years of blah, blah, blah." The AC Matrix would put her in the High-High quadrant, both for Emotion and Conviction. She was outright audacious and correct: **the science did not lie**.

Greta's audacity was not mere lip-service. Committed to not travelling by air, she journeyed on a sailboat for two weeks to attend the 2019 UN Climate Action Summit in New York. This credibility may be another reason why world leaders and celebrities – former US President Barrack Obama; The Pope; King Charles III; United Nations Secretary-General of the United Nations António Guterres; Scotland's First Minister Nikola Sturgeon; Austrian Federal President Alexander Van der Bellen; even actors Arnold Schwarzenegger and Leonardo DiCaprio, amongst many others – sit up and listen to her, and happily have their pictures taken with her.

The overarching question here is: regardless of audacity being positive or negative, **does being audacious pay?**

Does It Pay?

"The first quality that is needed is audacity," is a quote attributed to early 20th Century British Prime Minister Sir Winston Churchill. "Success is the child of audacity," is a quote attributed to his predecessor, 19th Century British Prime Minister, Benjamin Disraeli.

Of the two, Winston Churchill has had his name in more ranking lists, including most popular, most powerful, or the greatest of British Prime Ministers. Based on what we gather from reliable news and biographical sources, it seems that his audacity paid off.

Greta certainly has "that" first quality of audacity, as evidenced by her "How dare you?" speech. Her road to success will likely take much longer, as we are nowhere near addressing the climate emergency.

However, does Greta's audacity pay? Let's have a look.

1. Cause: A young Swedish girl is enraged that not enough is being done to mitigate climate change. She takes it upon herself to be a global voice to rally the youth. She sits outside the Swedish Parliament for three weeks until election day, insisting on more action for climate change. This is followed by a regular "Fridays for Future" (FFF) strike to protest climate issues.

Effect: Greta's determination snowballed into a global movement. Within months, more than 17,000 youth from 24 countries were doing the FFF school strikes. Within a year, this swelled to two million people across 135 countries. The beneficiaries of Planet Earth – the youth – rallied into action through her courage and tenacity.

2. Cause: World leaders were challenged and taunted with harsh words by Greta. Operating mainly from the High-High Quadrant, with conviction and emotions both high. This contributed to her being fearless, disrespectful, and insolent. She spared no one in reminding them that their climate platitudes were "30 years of blah, blah, blah" that had not led anyone anywhere nearer to a solution. The Atlantic wrote that "...her speeches take a shaming, authoritative tone... unusual for a child."

Effect: With the overwhelming international media attention on her, Greta's words travelled far and wide. The backlash was a given. Donald Trump advised Greta to work on her "anger management problem" and to "go to an old-fashioned movie with a friend". Vladimir Putin called her a "kind but poorly-informed teenager". However, others said differently. Sir David Attenborough remarked: "She's achieved things that many of us who have been working on it for 20 odd years have failed to achieve. That is you have aroused the world. I'm very grateful to you. We all are, really." Prince Harry said: "Whatever your dream – every country, every community, every school, every friendship group, every family needs their own Greta – someone who can lead the way, someone who is prepared to stand up for what they believe in, and show how much they care for the people in their lives and the community around them."

It's often said that there's no such thing as bad publicity. Greta's campaign definitely gained further traction.

Audacity: It pays.

We know that climate change impacts all of us, and that each of us is responsible for reducing greenhouse gas (GHG) emissions – but unfortunately, we all have differing levels of commitment. As such, when the world witnesses an unprecedented global wake-up call such as the one Greta gave us, it is a moment for gratitude.

It takes someone with audacity to shake the world and its leaders.

Greta has since been bestowed with a long string of well-deserved recognitions and awards. She received the Ambassador of Conscience Award from Amnesty International in 2019 – sharing the company of Nelson Mandela, who was a past recipient of the same award. In that same year, she was nominated for the Nobel Peace Prize, as well as being named *Time* magazine's *Person of the Year*. She was just 16 then, making her the youngest person ever to be chosen. Meanwhile, both *Forbes* and *Time* included her in their *100 Most Influential* and *Powerful* lists, respectively. In 2021, Greta was conferred an honorary Doctorate of Law by the University of British Columbia.

Appropriately, the accolades even stretch to the animal kingdom, where several species were discovered and named after Greta. For example, The Natural History Museum of the UK in 2019 named a new species of beetle from Kenya as *Nelloptodes gretae*, stating that "its long antennae bear a passing resemblance to her braided pigtails".

Greta could not have had the outreach nor attained what she did without being audacious. As they say: love her or hate her – but you can't ignore her.

Naturally Audacious

As I look back at how a person so young had the audacity to both enrapture and enrage the world, I reflect on my own journey in life. I recall several occasions when I had to step-up even though it did not seem like the popular position to adopt. My memory takes me back to something universally natural.

I would not have been exposed to audacity in its natural state until I conceived my second child. It was a difficult pregnancy. Somewhere in my second trimester I was informed by the doctor that I had Type Three Placenta Previa.

I had no idea then what this meant. The doctor explained to both my husband and me that there are four grades of Placenta Previa. A normal delivery is possible for Grades One and Two – but for Grades Three and Four, it will require a caesarian section. My first born was by natural birth – so to me, getting a C-section sounded disturbing. He then explained that Placenta Previa is a condition where the placenta is very low in the uterus – practically covering all or part of the opening to the cervical opening. Since mine was Type Three, it was partly covering the cervix.

Next came the seemingly difficult part – which doctors somehow seem to deliver with an expressionless face. He said that I would need to be totally bed-rested in the hospital until delivery – which meant just over three months in the hospital – as any movement could trigger fatal heavy bleeding.

The doctor's words deeply affected me. I felt hollow inside, imagining the worst. Since I was in a private hospital, he told me that to remain at this hospital for even three to four months would drain me financially, especially if there were any complications – which the medical insurance might cap or decline to cover. Following the doctor's advice, I shifted to a university hospital, and was assigned an obstetrician and anesthetist.

For me, it wasn't just about being stuck in the hospital, but about being totally confined to bed. I was only permitted to walk to the bathroom. A typical five-second walk to the attached bathroom would now take 30 seconds, as I was instructed to walk mindfully and haltingly. This went on for more than a month – by which time I already knew that I was having a daughter (Yippee!).

One day in my seventh month, I started bleeding. I managed to make a call to my husband while triggering the emergency switch. I was so used to the doctor's otherwise chirpy conversations; and now for the first time, I saw anxiety on his face.

Despite being propped up with oxygen, I felt weak and faint. I kept drifting in and out, with only one thought on my mind: "Please God, let my daughter be safe." Like Greta, I was practically fighting with "my world", challenging my eyes to remain open, my breath to remain constant, and my heart to remain strong. Nothing untoward must happen to my child!

I could hear the doctor ask his team to wheel me to the Operation Theatre since my pressure was fast dropping.

I felt cold, but just prayed – and even bargained with God that if He had no other option, then to please look after my daughter. As I was being wheeled away, my husband arrived. He passed me his phone: my father was on the line. He told me to not worry, and that all will be fine.

I repeatedly asked the doctor if my daughter would be alright, and to please save her. He ignored me – until at one point, he looked me straight in the eye and said bluntly: "My priority is to save you."

I was disturbed with his response. How dare he say that?!?

I was soon knocked out by general anesthesia. The next thing I knew, I was up and being wheeled back to my room. I was told that my daughter had been born prematurely and with a low birth weight – and that she would need to stay on at the hospital, and that I should come by daily to feed her.

She was home after two weeks. I had to feed her every two to three hours as advised. It was tiring – but there was the best way to strengthen her. Within a few months, she became better, gradually putting on some weight. It's been quite a journey as I look at her today, my lovely young lady.

Some weeks later, I learnt that when my husband called to inform my parents about my condition, my father had told him to convey a message to the doctor. My father's message was that if a choice had to be made between mother and child, then his daughter should be saved.

We both must have sounded crazy to the Creator up there.

This is audacity: Difficult choices, harsh decisions, good intentions.

Fortune Favours the Bold

by Norlida Azmi

At times, you get intimidated by the news or stories you read, causing you to draw a sharp breath and think: "Do my bold ambitions stack up to those doing bold actions for world peace, addressing hunger, inventing new innovations, or other "loftier" goals? Will my one audacious goal even matter?"

If your audacity is in the realm of doing community good, one single contribution can have a dramatic impact, prompting a quantum leap of progress to a wider set of people. It could impact national-level policies; it could save marginalised communities – to cite just a few possibilities. If your audacity impacts your personal being, it will empower you to do even more audacious things, over and over again.

There are some people who will ask: "What is the return on investment then?" If you want to answer that, you must remember that it's not always about money. It could be in terms of lives impacted; number of trees saved; or hours of counselling given. It is often difficult to quantify non-tangible results in a world with competing needs for resources – especially if you are asking from others.

We may need to understand how does being audacious pays – which it does. At so many levels.

Your boundaries are pushed

At times, you may have self-imposed limiting thoughts, based on previous experiences – or you and the people around you just say: "Get real!"; "Really?"; "It's impossible". These responses will then subconsciously push you to lower your standards of expectations. Sometimes, safe standards are a means of self-preservation, so as not to be disappointed or get hurt – and some people around you are also more comfortable if you don't go against the grain.

I believe you have to push yourself into areas of discomfort so that you can grow and achieve more. If you continue to operate within the same zone, your levels of achievement would not exceed the normal. So, if you are audacious and seem to ask for the moon, you may just get it – and if not the moon, at least the stars!

Thinking audaciously definitely takes our thinking out of the box – and your actions out of the normal ring.

When a husband-and-wife team work in the same organisation, the wife would "normally" be regarded in some companies as a "dependant", and not be accorded separate standalone entitlements. When my husband and I were peers at the CXO level at a bank in Qatar, I took up an audacious cause to bring about independent entitlements based on the role and not based as a dependant. This was way before I was consciously championing Diversity, Equity, and Inclusion (DEI); and I wanted to ensure that all female staff – from the lowest grade to C-Suites, regardless of marital status – were entitled to the same privileges as their male counterparts, even if they had spouses in other companies where they would be enjoying dependant privileges.

I wanted to make my choice. I wanted these other women to also be enabled to make choices.

I got the proposal through – and learning how to do it sparked my desire to drive parity in the workplace, no matter where I am. Pay and benefits parity remain till today an agenda that needs to be addressed in the diversity and equity campaign. To close that story: it did not mean that my husband and I used both our housing allowances to the maximum in order to rent a huge mansion – because we did not need, nor want, that 'bigger" house – but it was a psychological fulfilment of independence.

It was for professional acknowledgement.

You get what you want; you get what you ask for. Mostly, and most of the times – but it still remains true, nonetheless.

Your confidence is boosted

As your audacious endeavours result in successes, you will build greater confidence to aspire to higher goals and ambitions. You will dare to dream bigger, and to ask for more. You will feel emboldened, feeding this "courage" with your thoughts and your articulations. Your self-talk gets more positive – and as you think about that audacious goal, I bet ideas and solutions just whizz past your brain, causing your heart to pound faster. And you just *cannot* wait to get going.

Quick reminder: **do not overanalyse things**. Trust your guts, your instincts. Subconsciously, your mind has balanced the calculated risks that fit into your appetite and tolerance for the unknown.

At times, you may not have all the resources to go it alone; but with your conviction – and possibly by now, your reputation of credible audacious dreams and successes that precede you – you may want to, and *will be able to*, partner and collaborate with other people and other organisations to get closer to that audacious goal of yours. To get other resources aligned and committed with you, you will need to possess a credible track record – and it may be that they seek you out, rather than vice versa.

Can you imagine the snowball effect if you get all those collaborations to drive that audacious goal? It's likely to get bigger – and possibly achieved even faster, as different sets of people may have better access to wider networks and higher capabilities to address challenges.

> *"Self-confidence is contagious."*
> *– Stephen Richards*

As we saw in the last chapter, you often hear these days about "fail fast, and learn fast." It means that being audacious nowadays will not necessarily be met with disdain should you fail to get what you ask for – or at least, in the initial instances. If you fail the first time, you learn from it; you take these learnings, and you recalibrate your audacity-meter – most probably to "Up".

Sometimes, society still remains unforgiving – especially when realisation of those audacious goals seems so distant. This is where your conviction and personal core strength need to hold you stronger and keep you going.

I do feel, though, that we should know when to pull back – especially when more negative or adverse implications of your goals have been substantially presented. Maybe you were blinded by self-consumption – or worse, just feeding your ego. However, do not allow yourself to be bullied into compromising your audacious ask – or be talked out of it – if you are convinced that your viewpoints and position are solid.

Your impact is wider and deeper

As your audacious asks get bigger, you would want the impact to be bigger, either for yourself or for the larger cause. I believe that impactful leaders have some degree of audacity in them where there is minimal aversion to risk (if any at all), because they know they have a big win compared to the downsides and damages. You would hear often the phrase: "Ask for forgiveness, but not for permission" – because audacious leaders never ask for permission.

Leaders of organisations who have a strategic intent for the organisation – and, at times, industry – in their line of sight are able to zero-in on key goals and to galvanise the organisation towards those goals. These audacious leaders dare to dream big, and have powerful communication and influencing skills. They are able to bring about emotive connections – either because they resonate similar values within the wider organisation, or because they are very "empathetic" (a famously popular word, these days).

The worst from this spectrum of leaders would be those that have audacious goals just to fulfil their egos – and unfortunately, it may not always be easy to separate this class of audacious leaders, as they can be disarmingly charismatic.

Audacious leaders could also have a "halo effect". The people around them may be equally inspired and energised to be as audacious as they are – and in an organisation with a constellation of well-managed audacious leaders and influencers, the shift in the organisational culture and achievements could be very monumental.

It is one contagion we do not want to stop nor cure.

I had the good fortune to work for such a leader, who had the audacious vision to take a conventional medium-sized domestic bank to the standards of "banking as it should be", by modelling after a large global bank. This, in the highly-competitive banking industry for the country and region. Many people thought he was crazy, ruthless, and arrogant – **but he did it**. He brought in leadership that would not generally be attracted to such organisations, and accelerated programmes to change the bank.

In one of the measures of this goal, we went from being second last in terms of customer satisfaction to being Number 1 – for many years.

They say getting to No. 1 is easy (if easier is the word for it) – but staying No. 1 is more difficult.

Audacious dreams need audacious means – and to motivate the service centre staff, they were richly rewarded to drive them towards the goals. They worked like crazy – and smartly, too. They deserved those rich rewards – and the bank was transformed.

(The sustainability of that status for the bank is another matter, as leadership changes.)

It was interesting that during that period, the audacious leader created such an energising culture – and people were inspired to do better and be bigger. Inevitably, when a leadership change happened, and they took a more mundane approach, most of the energised leaders found alternative work. They were now addicted to drive, or to be part of corporates with **BHAG**.

You make a difference to yourself and to others.

You do more justice to yourself when you have the courage to live the life **you** want to lead – without any compromises, and without settling for second best.

I love Lady Gaga. I think she is visibly audacious in the way she packages herself: her clothes and her hairstyles set fashion statements and trends; her style of conversations and her advocacies brings transparency to sensitive issues; and her music is simply powerful. Even in movies, she takes on roles that have audacious personalities: it's like she is authentic about who she is at all times. **Her audacious self**.

I was also very taken by her openness about her journey when suffering and managing mental health issues arising from sexual assault, PTSD, and many other chronic pains. Audacious influencers like Lady Gaga are able to impact so many of the social, political, and environmental issues, with both their advocacy and their actions. Depending on your cause, I believe you need visible audacious symbolism to get the message across – and at times, getting attention is a good thing.

I reflect and think back to when my daughter told us that she wanted to step out of her corporate life and be an entrepreneur – and I had asked myself: when she wanted to live out her audacity that manifested in her dreams, did I provide enough support for her? I did – but not nearly enough. Even though I would assess myself as being high in spontaneity and desire for adventure, my instinctive reaction was one of caution. Driven out of love and a desire to protect her, I was scared for her. Was that it the right time? Entrepreneurship in bras? Is it really the right product? With so much competition, how will she succeed?

I am proud to say that over a short time, I understood her motivation. I understood her audacity. I became her number supporter – at least as her mother, I would like to think so! We cannot judge and evaluate from our experiences alone – particularly in a rapidly-changing world, where measures of success and pivotal experiences have changed. The next time she wants to do an even crazier thing, I am going to say: "Go for the maximum!"

I share this, as there are many ways in which we can drive audacity, and move the scale of courage to live our dreams higher.

Being audacious pays in so many of the roles that I have undertaken and that I am in. I must confess though that my appetite for audacity has increased as I grow older. It is not ambition alone that is driving this, but wider exposure and knowledge about so many more things. As you connect the dots, you have clarity of want you want to push and stand for.

How has audacity paid off for me? **In spades**. As a professional, wife, mother, friend, and member of the various communities I am in.

In all these instances, I have dreamed, and I lived courageously – and the journey still continues.

My husband always says this of me: "Throw an adventure at her, and she leaps at it!" Sometimes dangerous, I know – but always worth it. And I keep wanting more...

Where Small Steps Achieve Big Strides

by Freda Liu

Why does it pay to be Audacious?

No risk, no reward. If the word "audacious" still scares you, then maybe you should start with something simpler.

When going through the breakdown of my marriage, I remembered praying to God that I did not want to come out of this situation a bitter person – or as the shell of the person I could be. "Better, not bitter."

To this day, this still serves as my mantra.

I have seen many marriages that have ended miserably, where one spouse – usually the woman – becomes a bitter person. This was the kind of bitterness that spills into work, friendships, and family – and I did not want to be this person; that much I knew. That was the first vision of myself: to have come out of this situation stronger. It's just that I had no idea what this "better" person would look, or behave like – and I did not know where to start.

This to me would be the one big thing in my life that didn't go "as planned". "Life is what happens to you while you're busy making other plans," as John Lennon once sang. I had to take a serious look at my life, at who this Freda Liu is. Freda Liu, who supposedly had everything in control, and whose life was going as planned – or so she thought.

When the earth opened up and swallowed me, I realised that I also had not been living my life audaciously – or rather, not audaciously enough. When calamity strikes, you see two kinds of people: One who crumbles, and One who gets knocked down but gets up again. I don't know when in the last decade that I decided to live audaciously (with calculated risks) – but it had been a case of not wanting to only wait for calamity to strike before I lived authentically and audaciously.

The Butterfly Effect

This is taken from Wikipedia and edited. In chaos theory, the butterfly effect is the sensitive dependence on initial conditions in which a small change in one state of a deterministic nonlinear system can result in large differences in a later state. The term is closely associated with the work of mathematician and meteorologist Edward Norton Lorenz.

He noted that the butterfly effect is derived from the metaphorical example of the details of a tornado – the exact time of formation, the exact path taken – being influenced by minor perturbations, such as a distant butterfly flapping its wings several weeks earlier. The concept has since been used outside the context of weather science as a broad term for any situation where a small change is supposed to be the cause of larger consequences.

Simply explained, I like to call it the ripple effect. When you throw a pebble in a lake, it creates ripples. I have reaped many rewards because I have been audacious – and it's never because of the big steps, but because of the small steps. To the outside world, they may seem like things have happened overnight – but no, it was a series of small steps.

Again, I will share various aspects of my life which have led to the fruits of my labour –the really small steps, which I am proud of. No, not everything has to be about monetary gain – because feeding your soul is more important. It may not be for everyone; again, only you can determine what's audacious for you (and only you). Maybe you just want to work on one area of your life – for now. But let's start somewhere.

How Audacity has paid for Me

Let me begin with the spiritual side. I have been a child sponsor of World Vision for more than 20 years. I had heard about the organisation, and liked what it stood for: not just giving fish, but teaching the community to fish. They help develop villages to become self-sustainable by building infrastructure like water pipes and electricity grids, as well as teaching the means to earn an income so that the sponsored child gets to go to school.

It started with RM50 – and I increased the amount yearly to cover five kids. When one project "finishes" – they stop when the project is completed, or when the child turns 18 – they are then replaced by another child or community. I was not fussed about which result happened. It is not something I broadcast – but it is something I do feel passionate about. I believe education is everyone's basic right – and I wouldn't have gotten to where I am today if I didn't have a basic education.

I know that over the years, I have sponsored many children from across the world. Recently, World Vision appointed me as an advocate – and I saw a video of one of my children having reached 18, who was hoping to pursue a career in fashion design. It feeds my soul that my RM50

– which otherwise would have been spent on I-don't-know-what – was used purposefully to change someone's life.

Another aspect has been my fitness. Having seen my father pass away before hitting 60, I vowed to make fitness a part of my life. I still have bad habits, mind you – and I am working towards changing that. Historically, my family on my father's side has always had high blood pressure and diabetes – so, I don't want history to repeat itself.

I was not active in sports growing up – and my divorce made me take a long hard look at my life. Did I love myself? If I didn't love myself, how could anyone else? How do I make fitness a part of my life? Like with anything else, the answer is: small steps. The underlying reason was to feel good (as we all know, exercise gives us happy chemicals) – and secondly, I would look good (as confidence is always a good look).

It started with me doing bootcamp three times a week, and then signing up for my first 10K six months later. I wanted to work on my stamina as well. Trust me, there's nothing like finishing your first 10K – more memorable even than a marathon. Over the years, I have run in several countries like Croatia, Spain, Turkey (crossing continents), Australia, and Kazakhstan.

You do see a country differently when running, as opposed to being in a tour bus.

It took me five years before deciding to do a full marathon. I did it at the Gold Coast – and it was painful. But I am so glad I did it, and it's still a feather in my cap. What has been the outcome of all this? I am definitely fitter than I was 10 years ago. Exercise is now a lifestyle, and I am moving every day.

Another key aspect involved my family – and, specifically, asking them for help. A lot of the things I have achieved externally would not have been possible had I not had the support structure for me to pursue my passions and dreams. I am not a martyr – and I cannot even begin to do it all. The people who believe they can do it all are be in for a big surprise.

During the process of my separation, I asked my ex-mother-in-law to live with me to help raise my son. We had a wonderful relationship – and she knew I needed help as a single mother. She continued living with me, even though her son had moved out – because we had one outcome: the well-being of my son, her grandson.

Why did I do this? Because my son needed stability as a result of the separation. Because the assurance that Poh Poh was at home when he came back from school was necessary. Because that stability of having the same home and the same routine helped ease the pain.

Not everything had changed; my ex-husband was welcome to visit and come by anytime – because he would be seeing his mother, not mine.

Every year, my son would go on holidays with me and **both** his grandmothers, so that we would all have memories. Yes, it was audacious to ask my mother-in-law for help even though I had gotten divorced. The Wonder Woman who was my ex-mother-in-law has since passed – and I am still so grateful for her love and support. It meant that there are no regrets in that part of my life.

Beauty and the Benjamins

Now let's talk about money. According to US Bank, "women are less likely than men to talk about money with friends, use finance-tracking apps, and watch money-related TV shows." I find this is so true among a lot of women. If you don't fall into this category, **well done**!

This goes beyond just having a job and income: it's a hard look at your finances for now, and the future. If you're a married woman, chances are a lot of you would say your husbands take care of the finances. I have to say that I was guilty of that too. And we've all heard horror stories where the husband suddenly passes away and the wife has no idea how things are done or where all the paperwork is.

This is something I still struggle with – and maybe it's patriarchal – but I don't like talking about money. As such, my advice is to find resources and connections that speak to your financial needs, who can help you by making investing and the managing of finances less stressful (or maybe even fun!).

My financial concerns have changed over the years at different stages of my life. Recently, I hired a certified financial planner to understand what my needs are for the present and the future – and audacity means that I had to be asked hard questions as a single mother:

- Who will take care of me if something should happen to me now?

- Should I live to a ripe old age, will I have quality of life if I am healthy and if I am unhealthy?

- Will I have the resources and means?

- What is enough?

- Do I need to scale back my lifestyle?

If by asking these questions, you got terrified – great! Now, it's time to take action! If not, then you're blessed. But yes: have the audacity to ask the tough and real questions.

Worth more than Gold

Now let's talk about audacity in friendships. Motivational speaker Jim Rohn says that we are the average of the five people we spend the most time with. This relates to the law of averages, which is the theory that the result of any given situation will be the average of all outcomes. Take a close look at who you're surrounding yourself with. And yes, there have been some friends I have chosen to create more boundaries with – I'm sure you have examples too.

There was one individual who came into my life like a hurricane. Great fun at first – and then she started telling me about the drama happening in her life. Slowly but surely, it seemed to be never-ending – and it was always someone else's fault, never hers. I was pretty sure that somewhere down the road, **I** would become an issue too – and so, ever so slowly, I avoided gatherings with her. Why? Because I didn't have the head space nor the bandwidth to handle her. (I still don't.)

Yes, I had to be cruel to be kind – kind to myself, that is. Your friends really are your future. The implication is that you don't just need to be more deliberate about **who** you're spending the most time with; you need to be examining your entire network and its influence on your life. You need to know **where** you sit inside the larger network of your social community.

And so, I have pockets of friendships with different people. Make sure that you're spending time with people who are in line with what you want for your own life (preferably people "better" than you, so that it raises your average!). You're **not** just the average of the five people you surround yourself with: it's way bigger than that. You're the average of **all** the people who surround you. So, take a look around – and make sure you're in the right surroundings.

As we can see, audacity in the small things will give you invaluable rewards. You will reap what you sow. Don't look at audaciousness from only a financial/monetary aspect, even though we tend to do so by default. When done right, audaciousness in other areas of your life can actually help you propel in your career or business, knowing that the important things are taken care of.

Ignoring Naysayers in Order to Shine

by Bavani Periasamy

Being audacious pays; it's the willingness to take risks and go for what you want, even if it's not popular or easy. It's important to have a sense of self-worth, to know that you deserve the best. You need to be bold and take chances – even if it means doing something that people might not agree with or understand.

Audacity is about having confidence in yourself, your ideas, and your ability to make them happen.

Being audacious is also about having deep conviction and belief in what you are championing.

In one of my recent coaching sessions, I heard the word "wicked" being issued. This reminded me of another coachee of mine who jokingly once said: "I'm going to be wicked!" I looked at her again – and she said: "I am going to be wickedly audacious." I said: "Yay! Good for you! So, what are you going to do?" Thus was born the story of Liana (whose permission I got to share this story).

Liana is a graduate from one of the leading public universities in Malaysia, having obtained a Degree in Chemical Engineering. Truth be told, she's is one of those girls who love to explore the world, work with her hands, get her hands dirty, and watch the sun set while she's enjoying an ice cream. A village girl at heart, as she fondly calls herself: *gadis kampung*.

While everyone was rushing around putting in their applications to big and small companies, Liana, with her degree in her hands, was dreaming of staying right where she was in her little town in Terengganu, and earning money right there. And she wanted to make **lots and lots** of money (Her exact words).

This degree holder loved working with fabrics, and discovered that she had a flair with creating simple classic designs on cloths. That was when she decided: "I'm going to be wickedly audacious and make money from my home. In the thousands! More than an engineer should make as a fresh graduate!"

Liana had the idea of selling homemade designer *tudung*s (i.e. the head scarf worn by Muslim women), so she got a loan from her father and proceeded to buy several rolls of fabric. There already was a sewing machine at home which belonged to her mother – and which she got permission to use. Liana then cut up the cloth into the necessary pieces according to the normal tudung sizes before sewing the edges and fixing on some sequins.

The next step was promoting her wares on Instagram – and within the week, she had nearly 50 orders, thanks to university mates who wanted to show their support. The newly-minted entrepreneur created a poster advertising customisation services based on the customers' designs – for an extra fee. To her surprise, many took up the offered service, mostly for special occasions like weddings and graduation – where the ladies could get uniquely patterned and designed tudungs that were exclusive to them. All in all, this kept my coachee busy for six months – for which she earned a clean profit of RM4,000.

Not bad for a fresh graduate who just started.

But it wasn't enough. Now, Liana was restless.

"Why stop at *tudung*s? People need more," she thought. They want to feel special and unique – and that was an untapped market. With that, Liana opened up a service to add designs to people's own existing clothes and *tudung*s; all they had to do was send her the materials, specify the design (either the ones they had in mind, or have Liana come up with her own suggestions), and then pay for the fabulous results. This too, proved to be popular.

It led to my little protégé buying plain long blouse pieces and making designs for them too – another hit venture that eventually saw her needing extra help: Liana had to enlist help from the other young ladies of her village. They came to her house after school and started sewing – and she paid them for the work they did. Word spread, of course – as fast as it possibly could in a small *kampung*, which beats all known Internet speeds from the various telcos hands down, as we all know. Not only was business growing, other women started coming to Liana seeking employment: single mothers, stay-at-home mothers, and more.

At first, a deal with a local seller to get a few more machines plugged this unexpected employment gap which Liana helped to fill – but the business kept growing, and soon her home could no longer cope with the expanding business. It meant renting space in a shop to accommodate storage – and the business ended up taking over the entire floor space, with a workforce of 10 people working full time sewing *tudung* materials, affixing sequins, crafting designs on fabrics, and selling the end products.

The degree holder accidentally became a tudung tycoon from Terengganu with her very own couture boutique.

Looking back, I admit that was, indeed, wickedly audacious!

At a time where the unemployment rate of graduates was high, Liana did not think too much about it. She knew what she wanted: she wanted to earn a lot of money – and stay right home doing it. And she did it!

Unsurprisingly, her family were initially sceptical. They were full of pessimistic questions and concerns:

- "How many people would really want to buy *tudung* from you?"

- "How many *tudung* would a women need?"

- "Do you really think people would want to buy so much that you can make a living from this?"

- "You studied chemical engineering – and now you want to sell cloth?"

- "You have the opportunity to make changes and bring your family out of poverty – and you are not making full use of what you got."

True to her word of wanting to be wickedly audacious, Liana believed that this was what she wanted – and that she would give it a try before giving up. Initially, she had no idea business would bloom so fast (or even if it would bloom at all); but she knew she had to try it – because if she didn't, she would always be wondering about that alternate future vision of success, and probably regretting not taking the plunge.

While getting a chemical engineering degree was also a proud moment for a *gadis kampung* like her and her parents, Liana knew that she always wanted to be at home while the money rolls in. She didn't mind the hard work, of course – because she would be doing something she loved. There certainly was no shame in working on sewing machines and handling needles daily – and she was simply providing a service. Even more importantly, the money she made was halal, AND she was helping other ladies of various ages and social standings earn a living as well. That was enough for her – and she firmly repeated this conviction to anyone who asked.

Liana, too, had an obligation to help her parents financially, as she still had siblings in school. A regular engineer job was what everyone expected the young lady to get in order to help her parents. However, she stood firm and did what she wanted – and did even better than anyone in her village could possibly have expected.

Truth be told, Liana proved to be one of the very few among her batch that started earning income immediately after graduating; many waited and struggled for months – some, even years – to get a full-time job. **Being audacious pays**: Liana has proven it. Not only was she earning for herself, the first-time entrepreneur helped many other women in the process. I think she showed the other women that being audacious paid off, by allowing them to stand up for themselves and making coin through an honest and decent venture – even when many in the village did not look upon this situation favourably.

A lesson that all of us can take from the story of my friend, the tudung tycoon, is this: we all can have dreams and even believe in our dreams – but really, how many of us would be bold and daring enough to go and do by choice what we really want?

Wait, there's more to this story – a spin off, actually – with an even happier ending. Liana discovered some of the women who worked for her gave the bank account number of their husbands in which to transfer their earnings. Being a graduate and very savvy in technology, the tycoon was not too happy to see women not having their own bank account

– which meant they didn't have full access to their own money. She knew that the husbands would have control of the money that, after all, went into their bank accounts – and asking the women to go and open their own accounts could potentially cause a rift between the couples.

So, being the wickedly audacious woman that she was, Liana decided that audacity was called for: the boss "encouraged" her employees to start up their own individual sole proprietorship – which meant opening a business bank account. She then taught them how to issue her invoices so that she could pay them for their services.

Again, I have to admit it: I'm impressed! Liana's cunningness and imagination helped her workers go through an entrepreneurial approach in order to take control of their finances. The audacity not only to go after what she wanted herself, also for the women of the community she lived in – and in the process, empowering them in the process.

Liana's audacity was (and is) about being courageous and taking risks. It is about daring to be different, and not settling for the status quo as what was expected from her – and this is a quality that we all need in our lives. It is especially important for entrepreneurs, who are always on the lookout for innovative and creative ideas that can help them grow their business.

The audacity of this woman – who rather cheekily said she wanted to be wicked – is one that is worthy of praise and accolades!

It's fitting that when the British want to say "Cool!", they say: "Wicked!"

So Little to Give, So Much to Gain

by Fu-En Yee

WHY DO I WANT TO be audacious?

Hmm… to be honest, I had never thought about "why". I just "became" audacious, for three reasons:

- I had enough, and enough IS enough.

- I realised that the only one person who can really change things around and make the difference *without being at the mercy of others* is me, myself and I.

- I want to BE myself. I do not want to be like some other people who kept saying "I regret I didn't be this, or didn't do that. Or, I wished I had been this or done that."

I cannot even point exactly when I *did* start becoming audacious – but there were quite a few moments in my life that called for me to stand up and step up.

I can remember vividly the scene of my beloved grandfather asking me to promise him to protect the family **at all costs** when he is not around. On top of that, I must make sure the family stays intact – and I need to lead my siblings to complete tertiary education in university with flying colours.

From that day onwards, it sunk into me that I needed to rise above the discomfort, fear, and insecurities that I had during my childhood days. Just like any other kid, I would rather play than read books. Just like my friends, I would rather have little gatherings and do all the fun stuff together. Just like my "girl" friends, I would like to stay "small" and be protected by others.

But then, that would mean I will not be able to chart the "future" that my grandfather had wanted me to create.

At that point of time, I "had to" – and I thought that I **"needed to"**. So, I started to be audacious. Instead of just listening, following, and obeying my parents, teachers, and people who are much older than me, I had my own opinions, views, and stands.

My View Matters

Of all the why's, I would say that this is the most important one: to voice my opinion, and to make sure that my voice is heard.

I have seen – and continue to see – many people swallowing back what they wanted to ask or say, let alone doing what they truly want. To me, this spells "catastrophe" that itself builds into grudges, anger, disappointment, and even hatred. The more it builds, the worse it becomes when it explodes – just like an untreated tiny wound that has become a massive wound with pus and blood, that sadly ends up with the victim having to amputate the whole part because it is just too late to be rescued: the infection so bad it has started to affect the blood.

Super drama, yes – but a big avalanche can be caused by a small rockfall.

I had that experience before. In moments when I thought I needed to be brave, I was also struggling with what others were saying. The following are some of the statements that made me hold back my words in the past:

How old are you to think you know more than us?

We had done this before; it won't work. What makes you think you can work this out?

We have eaten more salt than you have eaten rice – a Cantonese saying which means the person has been around and gone through a great deal more than you.

All you need to do is listen and follow what we say!

You are too young to…

The more I swallowed and kept my words to myself, the more negative and unhappy I became – and the more I could not be "myself".

The most fundamental of being a living human is having the freedom to be exactly who you are. You have your dreams, your wants and needs, and your birth right and voice. No one can take these away from you.

It is only revoked when you allow it, when you surrender them to someone else.

Be clear though: I am not advocating never-ending arguments and raising endless conflicts. It is an art to communicate our views precisely, confidently, and firmly. Being audacious is not about being in control of others; being audacious is never about winning either.

It is about having the ability to articulate and express what matters to you.

It is about allowing others to know, understand, and respect you as a unique individual.

It is also the ability to accept the fact that there are – and that there will be – differences out there.

At the end of the day, **I matter. You matter. We matter as living beings.** If you give up voicing out your own opinions, wants, and needs – if you give up on your own dreams, then who else can be your true advocate for your interests? Who else will care about the differences you want to make in your own life if not you?

Build Confidence

Another brilliant reason for being audacious is that it builds confidence. The more audacious you are, the more confident you become. It will continuously spiral up, even at moments of doubts. Audacity helps to move things forwards and upwards, to the direction that you want it to be.

When I first learn to speak what was in my mind and others accepted my view, the voice in my head went: "Damn, that feels good! Why didn't I say so earlier?!?" I learnt to brave myself up to speak what's in my mind from that moment on.

If you asked me if all my views were accepted all the time? Well, obviously NO! There were moments when someone senior disagreed – or even being rubbished off – my ideas. At the very minimum, they teased me – but at least I had done my part in contributing my perspectives.

When things went wrong, I was more than happy to exclaim: "See! I told you so!" Well, that's just me being cheeky (which does not happen that often). But it reassured me that my perspectives were right, and strengthened the confidence that I had for myself.

What about if I made a mistake, where my views were not helpful, or even of no value to the other side? That becomes a **learning**. I did share in earlier chapters about audacity meaning embracing both the good and the bad, the strengths and weaknesses in me. The mistake became a learning on a specific weakness that I may need to work on. It gave me confidence that I am growing, becoming better, wiser, and smarter.

The more audacious I become, the more I can work on my weaknesses; the more that I can improve, the more I evolve – and the more confident I am.

Energy Sufficiency

I mentioned earlier that being audacious means embracing the whole of "me", both the good and the bad. In everything in life, there are always two sides to everything: yin and yang; left and right; up and down; give and take; pros and cons; positive and negative.

Try breathing out and continuing to breath out, and breath out – without breathing in, You can't, right? It doesn't work the other way around either.

There is no such thing as only having one side of things. I can go on listing the duality in everything, even as part of nature. We need two sides to see contrasts. It is only with that that we can learn to appreciate what is around us. The same goes for us as human beings. We are unique because we have our good and our bad. Our voice is sweet because we have both the high pitch and the low pitch.

Audacity: I am who I am. I mention upfront that what I cannot tolerate. I speak about what is true to me with compassion. Therefore, I communicate with ease. I never have to assert additional energy to think twice about what I had to say, and to whom. That enabled me to focus on creating outcomes that I wanted. There is no "energy loss" in the day, as my head is aligned with my heart.

I still remember back in the corporate days when there were certain duties that contradicted with my values. Logic and common sense told me that I need to fulfil those, as they were still part of my responsibilities. Clearly, there was misalignment between the heart and the head.

To deal with that dilemma and frustration, the body consumed a lot of my energy – and I often experienced a stiff neck and shoulder pains. Tiring.

However, since I have left those conflicting days, what I experience now that I am doing what I love is "flow". I no longer have dilemmas. My head and my heart are aligned, and there is endless energy in me to complete all the daily tasks. Practically, I become laser focused on what I need to do – and this itself allows me to achieve what I want so much faster and easier.

This is super crucial as we run our day-to-day schedules, carrying out significant duties as a daughter/sister/spouse/ parent/partner/friend/leader/what have you. If you could just pause for a while and take a closer look at those around you, do you see a majority of the people feeling exhausted even before mid-day – or are they fully energised till the end of day?

Obviously, the first group dominates the community. At the same time, you will also notice these are the people who aren't happy with their life. So much dissatisfaction, disappointment, and disillusionment. All these negative emotions zap away **A LOT of energy**. To avoid feeling these negative states, some chose to disregard the signals by numbing their hearts – something that actually makes things even worse. The fact is, no matter how intelligent or smart these people are, when the heart is disconnected, they always experience exhaustion.

Therefore, **having energy sufficiency is one of the best gains for being audacious.** I consider this as my best reward.

Calmness and Connectivity

In a survey done by Gallup in partnership with the Wellbeing for Planet Earth (WPE) Foundation in 2020, 72% of people across 116 countries preferred calmness over excitement in their lives. Only 16% would rather have an exciting life, while 10% wanted to have both.

This does not come as a surprise to me: in my experience as a psychotherapist, calmness *is* one of the wants most commonly quoted, aside from courage, happiness, and patience.

Like the broken record that I am, I believe that audacity means embracing the whole on us, both good and bad, while constantly working on the areas of improvements. How audacity promotes calmness is straightforward: **accepting our true self means we are comfortable in our own skin**. We are not concerned, worried, nor anxious about how others perceive our weaknesses – hence, there is no doubt and no necessity to put on a different mask to camouflage those weaknesses. We will be able to remain indifferent to what others see, say, or think about us – a calmness that many seek after.

That is why I also strongly believe that audacity is the best antidote for imposter syndrome.

People who can remain calm at all times are able to stay focused on the people, matters, and things around them. They can connect at a deeper level, as the energy is well focused, instead of spreading over to worrying and thinking about how to best present themselves in front of others.

From "I have to be audacious" and "I need to be audacious", I am proud to admit that **"I have chosen to be audacious"** – and that **"I want to be audacious!"**

Ultimately, all the above are some of the greatest gains for being audacious. I am 45 now, and I am delighted by the way being audacious has gifted me for my life.

CHAPTER 4
Beyond Audacity

A Discovery of Audacious Authenticity

by Syireen Rose

How is being the best version of me a true showcase of authenticity? Who's to know who I am and what I truly represent? What if being authentic means being a liar?

One of the most talked about dilemmas is the Imposter Syndrome. Loosely defined, it is when you doubt your own worth and accolades, and feeling like a fraud. Apparently, it affects more women than men – the high achievers who question their personal wins.

As much as there is call for us to stop telling women that they suffer from Imposter Syndrome, the more I study the cause and effect of this syndrome, the less I am able to deny that I, too, underwent systematic abuse of the mind and heart – so much so that I ended up broken and defeated, even though others seem to feel that I am a success.

As I search and search – while feeling like an absolute liar to myself and the people I lead – I am reminded of a mantra: "BE-DO-HAVE". Basically, the mindset is to visualise who I want to BE, and respond to situations exactly how I would, should I have become the BEING I have envisioned myself. In practicing the "BE-DO-HAVE", I would (in theory) show up 100% in the BEINGness of the person I plan to become; and eventually, in the process of doing – that is, by taking action – I will eventually HAVE what I envision to BE.

Definitely a mouthful – a chunk load to digest. And in all honesty: easier said than done.

Why?

I am a staunch learner, which led me to attend various self-development programmes. I have listened to folks saying that we ALL have a CHOICE – and to a certain extent, I do agree. At the same time, I am a witness of reality where I've experienced and/or watched the "grooming"/"conditioning"/"hypnotising" – and the many other tools and strategies used to control behaviours. I have read where women are repeatedly abused and taken advantage of; bullied and manipulated in cults and groups purportedly deep in either spiritual or transformational work.

Very disturbing – but true.

And, although I may not have undergone such trauma nor horrendous mental treachery, I won't discount my experience as less defeating or damaging to the soul.

In the previous chapters, I shared the various challenges I faced, and the means I took to overcome them. This chapter is about two follow-up questions: "So what?", and "What's next?"

I want to express what is possible beyond audacity. There may be many words, innovations, and conversations about breaking ceilings, the next giant step, going all out with everything that you've got, etc. – and yet, despite all the audacity, your life is by your design.

What do you really, really want for you?

I trust that the true audacity is living by choice and always in response to what is present. Letting go of the past and essentially being complete with it – not to be paralysed by the thought of the future that we cannot control nor which may never come. Audaciously, I shall declare that I am not a believer of details in planning, but I believe in making a big picture plan: not to dictate my life, but to give me direction.

I acknowledge that there is no going forward with no aim – and at the same time, we know for a fact that life throws curveballs. So, I put it to you that the audacity in living, in my opinion, is responding to the present: living and making decisions in the now, no matter what the initial big plan is.

For the highly compliant and for those who need stability, maybe this approach won't work so well – and that's exactly the point of audacity. It's a conversation of courage that is enveloped in doubt – but driven by commitment to take action. By design. Being in high awareness of our thoughts, feelings, and actions is key – and it's okay to not get it right at every decision.

Life is a series of practices towards the achievement of mastery. For a go-getting dominant personality like myself, I am forever driven – but I refuse to be boxed in by any definition of SUCCESS. This uncertainty irks many – and I have come to a point in life that I stop apologising for not fitting in to other people's reality boxes.

I just know I have a plan to succeed, and then I decide every day by answering the simple questions like: "How do I respond to today?"; "How would I like to show up today?"; "In which essence of my BEING will I focus on today?" – and with that decision of BEING will be the choices that I make with the opportunities presented daily.

I often leverage on the available resources and knowledge that I have gathered, and take leaps of faith. I am busy living and designing SUCCESS on my own terms so that I don't box myself in. I resonate with Buckminster Fuller about circles – because when I draw a circle, I, too, can't wait to step out of it.

It is not that I don't care about what others think, or feel, or need to feel safe; I simply believe that I need to begin with myself. I need to be 100% in my integrity and authenticity to be of value to the world around me. Should I not be focused on a complete me, then I will have nothing to give others. What am I worth when I am not giving back?

Having said that, the "I" in my conversation is carefully evaluated so that the EGO does not overtake the conscious decision to care for me and make it a selfish endeavour. I often hear people say: "It is my choice not to do it, because I need to take care of myself." – but at the expense of others. I can't do that – nor do I agree with such statements, because in all honesty, my key success lies in others succeeding with me. How can we deny doing and participating in life when those activities impact others living with us? You see, I love caring for others – because nothing is about me.

However, I have learned that I cannot function for everybody, and for the world as I wish it to be. Often, the outcome I experience from the world is what the world makes it to be. But I can make a difference for individuals who receive and welcome my work. Only that part of my work matters – so I focus on it, audaciously. My passion to share knowledge and add value is my trump card in life.

Neither I nor you can ever Google Search for the category we fit nicely into – and still, I am okay to put myself on the hook, stand in the heat, and make a promise. I will always be in my passion: the Power of Words in leadership, in networking, in wealth creation, and mostly, in the BEINGness of an individual – but I cannot take anyone anywhere, because no one will follow.

I can only invite – and I allow what comes with it.

I often declare that I am merely a conduit; nothing that I have, I own – hence, I am here to earn permission with the gift of wisdom that **He** flows through me for those who need it and who want to gain access to it. I am never inaccessible, and always open to talk (within reason). I keep working on serving – even when I am least heard, ignored, and neglected in my plight. And when people come up and say: "I want to follow you.", then I know I am on my way to contributing everything I have – and everything I am – with everything I am born to do, audaciously.

I know now – after all my years of bruises and learning – that leadership is within me. Though the fear and doubt to stay in excellence remains, I will stay committed to taking action for others to benefit from my existence. Everyone is seeking a solution in their lives – and I hear them daily in their choice of words.

When you speak to me, I most likely will hear you too – so, why not speak?

Finally, my invitation is for everyone to stop living in other people's expectations:

- Get clarity, and function in your brilliance.

- When lost, ask for support – because there is always someone who will help.

- Don't feel defeated when one team abandons you: they are not the best fit. Find the team/friends/comrades who truly appreciate your worth.

- Everyone is worthy – so, are you? He does not make mistakes.

You are a gift from **Him**: the missing piece that the world is waiting for. Don't rob us of your brilliance.

Audacity Begins with "I"

by Sharma Kumari

The Seed

When I was seven, I attended school for the first time ever at Standard 1 in the Methodist Girls' School (MGS). Back then in the 1960s, kindergarten was not the norm, unless one came from the upper income category. Nevertheless, having six older school-going siblings meant that I had the advantage of being able to already read and write English. It also meant that as the youngest, I had mastered the art of being heard by speaking several decibels above the normal range.

An all-girls school, MGS was also the place where I fell in love at first sight. This person came to school in a swanky red MG sports car. Each morning, I was given the honour of waiting for her, to walk ahead of her, carrying her books into the staffroom, sometimes helped by a classmate. This was my first formal teacher: Mrs. Yeoh. Tall, attractive, with impeccable *cheongsams*, a most kindly voice, and a radiant smile. She would even call upon me or the classmate to ring the school bell for recess on most days. Power to the hungry!

In the early months, Mrs. Yeoh divided the class into two batches. She then called upon me, and asked me to teach one batch to read the letters of the alphabet, while she taught the other batch basic word construction. Mrs. Yeoh's induction method was simple: She handed me a ruler, and told me to point each letter as I said it aloud, before letting the rest follow me. Without batting an eyelid, I went up to the board and started "teaching" A, B, C, right up to Z, and then repeating the lesson.

In addition to English and the Malay language, Mrs. Yeoh also recognised that I could speak Punjabi. She had another task lined up for me. I had a fellow Punjabi classmate (I do recall her name) who hardly knew a word of English nor Malay. Mrs. Yeoh now appointed me as an interpreter. For every sentence she spoke, I would turn to my classmate and ask her the same in Punjabi, listen to her response, and interpret it right back into English for Mrs. Yeoh.

Over time, Mrs. Yeoh and I amused ourselves each time the interpretation was needed. Instead of me doing the opening lines, Mrs. Yeoh would sometimes start off the conversation with the exact words I used by saying: "Teacher *kehndi…*" ("The teacher is saying…") before passing the reins back to me. Even my Punjabi classmate would giggle at this each time. By now, I was also an ad-hoc "private tutor" to her, especially for the other subjects taught in English.

Towards the end of the year, four students were picked from our class to perform at the Primary 1 school concert. I was amongst them, and was to be the Indian "doll" amongst the other Chinese, Malay, and Japanese "dolls". I love dancing – and this was the highlight of the year for me. The bonus from this was getting a special new outfit for the performance, sewn by my mother.

What happened next was totally blue ocean for me. Just a few days before the concert, Mrs. Yeoh told me that I will be announcing the class item during the concert. I had no idea what this entailed. She patiently wrote me a script to introduce our performance – which mainly included a salutation, our class name, the title of our performance "Let's pretend to be a Doll!", and ending with something like "hope you enjoyed the performance."

It was only during the concert that I realised Mrs. Yeoh was personally announcing all the other concert items. I had audaciously done my first ever emcee gig. As I think back to that day, I do not recall declining, nor feeling nervous – and certainly not even wondering if I was perhaps *supposed* to be anxious.

We know that at any one point in time, we are the sum of all our experiences and thoughts in our life. These will continue to shape us. Until this point, I had never deeply pondered on these "firsts" instilled by Mrs. Yeoh. As I look back, I now consider her every request as a display of confidence in me. I regard this as the integral audacity seed germination stage.

The Growth

I am certain there could have been audacity-presenting instances when I was even younger which I am unaware of. Let me focus on when I started school.

During my first few days at school, I witnessed many other students crying when they had to go into the classroom, or when their parents were not in view. Some of these parents had to be around for almost a month. Was it the audacity of confidence when I could tell my mother that I would be fine, and that she did not have to be with me every day? I reckon, this must have been due largely to the normalisation of daily school-going rituals amongst my siblings.

Beyond that, I do see how Mrs. Yeoh's various requests had inconspicuously, but audaciously, contributed to some of my actions and decisions made in later years. For example, having "taught" my contemporaries their ABCs in Standard 1, I did not flinch when a neighbourhood lady approached me to give English tuition for three months to her three young children. She offered me the princely sum of RM20 a month (equivalent to RM120 today)!

I audaciously accepted, not even anticipating the challenges before me. I was excited – both by the "pocket money", as well as the fulfillment gained from helping someone learn. Their ages ranged between 6 to 10 years, or so. They all attended a Chinese-medium school and spoke only Cantonese at home; I was 12 years old then, and barely knew Cantonese. What was I thinking?!?

This gig as a "paid professional" turned out better than I expected. Since they had no choice but to converse with me in English, the kids generally made good progress. The two sisters were more dialed in than their "cheeky" brother, who would burst out laughing at anything and everything. Funnily, he was the one who kept the sessions lively.

What I learnt from this teaching experience was to be accepting of different kinds of learners as they contribute to the rhythm and healthy "competitiveness" of learning.

Moving forward, I adapted to their need to have an overview of the lesson of the day with a summary recap at the end.

This experience, and several more in the years to come, contributed the layers towards how I would then run my current training and consulting outfit. Audacity certainly pays over and beyond.

Speaking of being paid: shortly after the three-month gig and RM60 richer, I eagerly dragged my mother to the popular local watch shop and indulged. I then proudly wore the fruit of my very first salary at age 12: a Swiss-made Stema watch. This was the start of my fascination with watches, which led to a collection of some 15 watches over the years (until smartphones made them somewhat redundant).

If I view taking on the tuition gig as being audacious on my part, I would be justified to consider Mrs. Yeoh's selection of me as concert announcer audacity on her part. Through both these unrelated events, my confidence to speak and connect with audiences grew. My relationship with the microphone – which started at such a young age – grew steadily over the years. It became my "voice-amplifier" during various school and university events, mainly speaking, announcing, debating, and play-acting.

Years later, this concert announcer was spotted and asked to audition as a television newscaster at the national network.

I was selected, and served as a part-time professional TV newscaster for more than a decade. Beyond that, I continue to serve as speaker, announcer, emcee, moderator, and anything voice-related (barring singing, of course).

I believe these may not have happened if not for the audacity kick-start by Mrs. Yeoh.

And Beyond...

All that I share are reminders to myself – which I hope will also resonate with you, dear reader.

In the earlier chapters, I shared various manifestations of audacities that we may have encountered: the audacity of hope; pessimism; suspense; desperation; empathy; purpose; challenge; authenticity; love; and more.

Audacity is doubtlessly associated with boldness, confidence, or self-assurance displayed through our speech or action when taking risks, facing difficulties, being adventurous, or challenging norms. It is viewed as being positive or negative, depending on which side one is on (the challenger, or the challenged).

Audacity grows within us through our various experiences. It is the bedrock of change. Beyond audacity is our trajectory and growth, giving our future actions the propellors they need.

From a very young age, I disliked and did not appreciate the need to wake up early. I can confidently assert there are others amongst my seven siblings who feel the same. I still recall once when my sister Kanti requested my mother to wake her up the next day, in case she didn't hear the alarm. My mum naturally said she would – and asked what time that would be. The minute Kanti said: "9am.", I still recall the priceless expression on my mum's face, as she remarked: "You need an alarm to wake you up at 9am?!? The neighbourhood kids have all showered, and are up and about by 7am!"

That's an audacious comparison, of course. As children are wont to do, we too did not quite cherish this comparison. However, as it was used often enough – coupled with my mum's non-disparaging tone – it was easy to avoid getting offended or scarred for life. However, it was still something that had further layered our life experiences.

For me, beyond audacity is about going past and beyond the literal words used. **There is the need to pause, step back, and to understand the intention.** So, when my mother made that neighbourhood kids comparison, I can assume that Kanti must have had the same light-hearted thought as mine right then: "What weird neighbours!" (They were not.)

Within ourselves, we both knew it was an indirect plea to instill the change she desired: for us to get up earlier in the mornings. Not immediately – but change did come about. That audacious sounding message did contribute to our trajectory for growth, with respect to waking up earlier.

We did not totally abandon late nights nor late mornings; it just meant we recognised the benefits of doing so when the occasion demanded. This would not have happened as easily – or at all – if my mum had not been audacious in her own way. Just imagine, if she only ever said: "Please wake up early." Over time, that mantra would have no bite – like an alarm clock perpetually on snooze.

Chicago screenwriter and producer Sylvia L. Jones challenges us to be audacious when she asks: "If money weren't a factor, if fear weren't a factor, if what people think weren't a factor, what would you want to do with your life?"

Interestingly, I know someone who checks all those boxes in Sylvia's challenge. This is what he has done – and continues to do – with his life: "Caring for the family, worked in a prawn factory, taught in a tuition centre, thought about a part-time job in a *thosai* shop, and worked in a mangrove swamp. Also played hard, studied smart in school and university, kept the grades up, got a job, worked with integrity – and years later, became the CFO of a *Fortune 500 Company*, till today."

He relentlessly took the path less travelled, was adventurous, and made bold choices: **Audacity**.

As I look back objectively, if I am confident, able, or successful in several aspects today, it is thanks to the audacity of those whom I approached to correct and guide me. Also, to those who chose to bite the bullet (to the detriment of our relationship), as they sincerely encouraged and accepted the authentic side of me – yet unconditionally accepting me in totality. A big shout-out to my significant other, my siblings and our respective families on this one!

I often reflect and wish, too, that some others had the audacity to call me out and tell me where they saw me drifting and failing. Their audacity could have me avoid missteps, wrongdoings, and misjudgments – just as I, too, should have done so with some whom I could have been more audacious with.

Many of us have positive self-illusions. The audacious approach – having the courage to say, and having the courage to listen – is a great reality check to cast off these illusions. However, as covered in the earlier chapters, audacity suffers from bad press. It is a greatly misused word.

There is a dire need to go beyond these misconceptions.

Let us move beyond – by socialising audacity for its intention and authenticity. We need to work collectively to generate a clear understanding of the term, its various forms and corresponding narratives. People should feel psychologically safe to show their authentic selves – to speak with audacity towards constructive and real goals. There should be no room for regret of not having spoken up for fear of reprisals.

At the end of the day, we should be able to look ourselves in the eye and say: "I trust I."

Staying True To Your Audacious Goals

by Norlida Azmi

The limits to your prowess and courage have now been defined by you. How far do you want to run, and how high do you want to soar? Beyond audacity, it is important to ensure you remain true to the cause – and to remain on course.

Imagine yourself as the artist, looking at the canvas of your masterpiece. The objects on the canvas are your dreams – the audacious ones, and the not-so audacious ones – and the colours that you use are the feelings and experiences you have chosen to pursue. The brushes are the courses of actions that you have taken to achieve that masterpiece.

Reflect Back

As much as it would seem impetuous, I feel that after that initial step when we take on an audacious course, we get more deliberate as we go forward, in both our thoughts and actions. So, the point beyond audacity is when you are able to stand back and see that you have been true and authentic to yourself – that your core has become stronger. What are these traits of yours that you feel have been sharpened and deepened? Your boldness? Your values? Which of these traits of yours have you dropped or lessened? Was it your need for universal acceptance? Or your fear of rejection?

It's like doing a Marie Kondo on yourself: you thank the parts that have carried you through in the past, and retain the parts that are going to carry you forward into the future. I enjoyed doing a Marie Kondo on my clothes and other belongings – so when I started applying it to my emotions, it gave me the same liberation. It was not as easy as with material things, and it is still an ongoing journey – but once you start, you get very efficient at it. The emotions that come from separation may still have the same intensity, but you have learned how to handle them.

You do learn "new" emotions – or more accurately, you learn to feel more comfortable with these new emotions; things like the ability to feel big, or to flex now that you are very good at something, because people want to associate with people who deliver; people who can win.

At this stage, I am reminded of the outcome of meditation that is called "luminosity", where amidst the unlimited variety of thoughts, feelings, sensations, and appearances that continually emerge in the mind, you have clarity about what matters to you. "Manifesting", as Gen Z would say. I am not a practitioner as I am impatient – but I often hear my two daughters citing the clarity they get from meditation, and am tempted to be more disciplined. Because getting clarity – no matter how you get it – is important to keep us driving towards our goals. This is especially true for complex audacious goals: the delayering of the challenges or issues associated with it may cause you to falter or take a wrong step next. **Clarity is like your North Star: it takes you back on course**.

Are you able to segregate or differentiate between your various goals? If you are like me, you want to do everything today and **now**. This aspiration sets an unnecessary pressure on ourselves, and could impact our total wellbeing and confidence. I heard the term "the world of overwhelm" – and we must not self-impose this overwhelm upon ourselves. As you evaluate your goals, think: are they all "audacious" – or are some more "normal"? (This is full appreciating the fact that "normal" is relative from one person to another, of course.)

It is important to be able to differentiate, as you may need to channel different levels of energy and resources to the audacious goals as opposed to the non-audacious goals. I feel that if you have too many audacious goals going on at any one time, you may not be able to focus enough energy and efforts to make sure it is successful – which leads me to talk about prioritisation. Which of these goals matter most to you today, when some of them could be done tomorrow and mean more then? At times, these goals are sequential, or stacked up so that you can spread your attention and efforts towards you can achieve these goals more seamlessly.

When you are pursuing your audacious goal, do you have a structure? How do you do your check-ins and checkpoints? (I don't mean you need to prepare a super scientific Gantt chart – although if that rocks your boat, go for it.) Is there a mental mind map that you navigate from? Use a structure that suits how you track and measure your audacious goals – and in your own style. I hate complicated things, so I chose the simplest method I can get away with, though it depends on the complexity of the goals and what other resources I have.

(I am not lazy – I just don't want to do unnecessary things.)

And by now, you would have shrugged off all the irrelevant expectations of the people around you, along with those toxic vibes and energy that would have pulled you down and held you back. More importantly, you would have identified your saboteurs and understood their motivations and actions so that you could navigate accordingly. This is not to say that you don't respect nor value these inputs and opinions – or at least, some of them – but as you are unpacking, you have been able to take on what matters. *This* is also where you close ranks with the sages and those that support you.

Overall, some of these opinions matter some of the time and in the right proportions – but your opinion is what ultimately matters.

A lot can be said about lessons learnt so that you don't repeat the same mistakes, and you can adopt the *modus operandi* that works best. However, at times, the same cause of "mistake" will not always cause the same outcome – so we must not generalise too much, or we will be numb to the full experience.

It could translate to too much caution, causing us to brake too hard. So, whilst lessons learnt are important, please temper your considerations into your audacious acts. Audacious goals have a certain rawness to them that keeps that hunger in you.

Charge Forward

Allow yourself to fully experience the joys and frustrations of pursuing these audacious goals, be they positive reactions or negative ones; that connectedness of your emotions and your actions and the outcomes – whether they are the final destination or milestones – is important. Some scientists suggest that emotions are critical for cognitive development and sustained learning – for memory, decision-making, and creativity. So, if you are going to remember the lessons learnt, you must feel the journey.

In charging forward, you need to have your tank full, with replenishments coming from many sources. What are the critical ingredients for success? From yourself: that grit and perseverance, as well as continued conviction. From others: keeping those people that matter close to you either to cheer you on or to provide counsel.

At this point, let's focus on the fun part of being audacious: injecting audacity into your attitude and personality! Be the one that says the most out-of-the box statements; the ideas that gets eyes rolling; or suggestions that could simultaneously suggest that you are out of your mind – because you could be the one that provokes the wildest idea, as you push your own thinking and that of others collectively to take the audacious route.

Illuminate your uniqueness and your special talent. How do you make yourself and your audacious purpose be special and stand out for the rest of the crowd? Achieve that, and it will make people care more; this essential for success and – at times – survival.

Audacity for you, and for me

1. Review, Refresh, and Regenerate your audacious goals

We all know the world has changed, and that different elements need to be incorporated to make it more relevant and more impactful. As a strong advocate of DEI (Diversity, Equity, and Inclusion), I have consciously elevated it within the topical issues of ESG (Environmental, Social, and Governance) – not because it trendy, but because in that space the interconnectivity across the globe and its communities is more pronounced, in addition to the accountability and transparency being higher.

Shifting your perspectives allow you to see if the mountain that you want to scale is actually the one you intended to. Realising that this is the wrong peak only at the *end* of the climb would have wasted your passion and resources. As you reset your personal and professional goals, you should seek to break your cycle of safety, comfort, and complacency. As you elevate your business and operational goals, you should swim across all the blue and red oceans – and seek to innovate, adapt, and future-proof your business.

How big do you want your audacious goals to be?

Who do you want to serve or benefit from this cause?

How will you deliver, and – possibly – compete and win?

2. Strengthen your Core, and Align them to your values

Strengthen your creativity muscles and your learning muscles, alongside having the physical strength to drive and persevere with your goals. Build up that toolbox of IQ (Intelligent Quotient), EQ (Emotional Intelligence), DQ (Digital Intelligence), and CQ (Cultural Intelligence) – and so many more capabilities.

Increasingly, value-based leadership has grown in importance – so your authenticity and capabilities are going to very apparent. Amongst your believers are the people that are going to benefit from your cause; imagine the hope and trust they have vested in you.

Manifest your leadership identity.

3. Define the Process, and Set the Timeline and Measures

You are executing with intent – so executing for results by a targeted timeline will bring greater focus and credibility. As mentioned above, the key to execution is your planning process: a clear working gameplan that has been designed to execute, as opposed to one that tries to create a perfect plan. With targets and milestones, you can adjust your actions more effectively. You've got your eyes on the horizon, true – but as you move towards it, you are likely to be doing a few dance steps, and demonstrating versatility.

> *"You've got to eat while you dream. You've got to deliver on short-range commitments, while you develop a long-range strategy and vision, and implement it. The success of doing both. Walking and chewing gum if you will. Getting it done in the short-range, and delivering a long-range plan, and executing on that."*
>
> *– Jack Welch*

4. Just Do It

My favourite tagline of all time (Nike has no idea how much this continues to impact my life), and my *modus operandi* since forever. You can never perfect a concept intellectually just in your mind: you have to get going; take away things in the process; add in between; and do whatever is necessary in between. Refine it as you go – and stay alert for actions by competing actions that could sabotage or marginalise your impact.

You may have a team or a group of friends – but it must be you that carries out the audacious goal strategy. Audacious leaders own it; they must **never** delegate some components of the execution, which at best is termed "strategic micromanagement". At times, we must run contrary to the dogma that leaders should stay out of the details and delegate for others to do it. There are just some parts where we must take charge and get our hands dirty.

Action and accountability.

Execute and Deliver the Results.

5. Repeat

So, you have the winning formula: Do you want to do more? And do you want to do it again?

My early computer programming basic algorithm says:

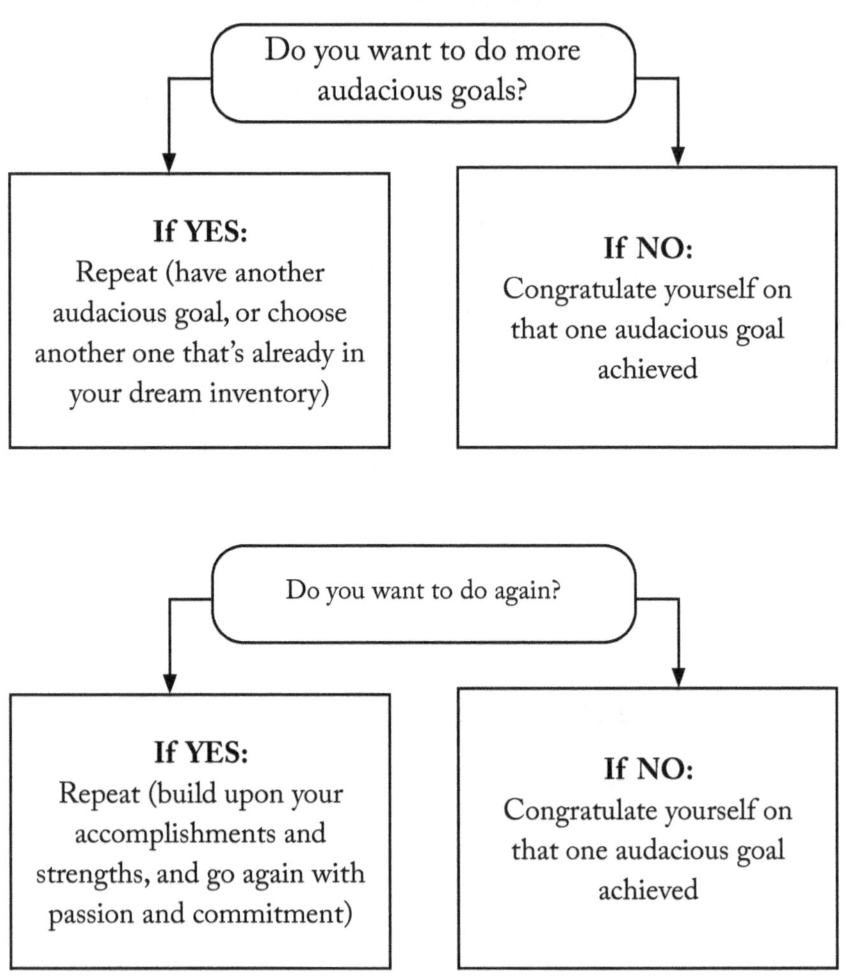

So: REPEAT, if you want to continue on the journey to be an audacious person / audacious woman / audacious wife / audacious partner / audacious professional / audacious leader.

Dare to live life to the fullest and making an impact with your audacious goals.

Patching the Missing Spokes in Your Wheel of Life

by Freda Liu

"**I** think it's interesting," my almost 20-year-old son Jude said. I believe it was a conversation about accommodation as he prepares to go on campus next year in Sydney. It's been a headache to get his passport, because he couldn't get an appointment to get his eyebrow ring removed – which meant he couldn't get his passport photo done.

Yes, I don't know whether to laugh, to cry, or to scream.

My baby is now his own man, and has to make his own decisions. As much as I would like to tell him what to do – because "Mother knows best!" – I am probably the last person he wants to listen to at this stage; his friends and peers being more important. There's nothing like your own children to keep you humble in case you ever thought that you had "made it" in the outside world – because everyone listens to you **except** your own offspring.

So, what do you do? You learn to let go. I have to trust the fact that I have guided him as much as possible – and that he then has to make his own decisions, and that his mother is always there to back him up.

Boy, typing that was difficult to do.

I pondered hard on this topic. What do you do beyond audacity?

I think it is the courage to not have all the answers – sometimes coming to the fact that the plans we have may not work out as planned – and that it's OK.

Now, learning to let go is not a case of "Que sera sera: whatever will be, will be" or a laissez-faire attitude about things; it is about **knowing** you have done your best – and believing that the best will come out of it.

Yours truly, by nature, found this very challenging to accept for the longest time. For those of you who know me, I am a striver: I strive and strive and strive. Maya Angelou said it best: "You want me to do something, tell me I can't do it." Nothing drives me like someone telling me I can't. This inspirational quote works for me.

That said, I also have to be wary of **why** I do the things I do. Is it because it's something I want to do – or because it's a case of one up(wo)manship? The latter is never healthy – and you will lose steam if it's not from within.

Know Thyself

I recently hosted a session with *New York Times* bestselling author and Global Peace Ambassador Prem Rawat just before writing this chapter. (Serendipity? Never!) His message of peace is a peace that can only come within. Let me extract some major thoughts from the book *Hear Yourself: How to Find Peace in a Noisy World*.

"Sometimes, the pressure is put on ourselves – and sometimes, it's put on by other people with their expectations. Ambition is good, but not when it stops us from experiencing the full richness of life. **Some of us are so busy trying to be successful that we don't get time to enjoy who we already are.** Some of us are so busy trying to get somewhere that we don't see where we are right now. Just like the Wi-Fi, we are 'always on.'"

Everything is temporary in the living world – our highs, and our lows. As I am writing this, the washing machine door is stuck, and I am trying to remain as calm as possible. In this immediate moment with no one at home, I am blaming everyone from the son to the ex-husband, and why the helper has to go away for a week.

(Yes, I was having an argument with an inanimate object. Very classy, Freda…)

And to think I was just reading in the book by Prem Sawat that says that everyone else can be the main characters of the drama in your life – partners, family, friends, colleagues, celebrities, politicians, even strangers – but you have to keep putting yourself at centrestage. (Not in an obnoxious sense – but in a humble sense.)

Why does the Noise of Life so often drown out the Music of Life? Because we can forget what's important. Let me practise this fact right now as I am writing, by going back to that washing machine: "I do have a washing machine that works. Hey, I own a washing machine. What a luxury!"

How petty of me to be having an argument with the washing machine!

This whole notion of knowing oneself – how often do we sit down in reflection of who we really are? Most of us can say what we're not – but not who we really are. It is still a discovery process for me. When we truly know who we are, it'll be a lot easier on the decisions we make in life – both in work, and at home.

Crossroads and Reflections

As I am writing this, it's nearly the end of the year – and I usually make goals for the next year right about now (in fact, I would have started on some of them). In fact, I also started this concept of scripting where instead of just writing goals, I actually script out how my day would turn out, and then I will see if it pans out at the end of the day. It goes on to ask us to write 10 days in advance, adding a few goals – and even wants and needs – that you aspire to achieve and acquire.

It's been quite uncanny with some things. Reticular Activating System (REM), simply put, helps you put things in focus – like only seeing red cars when you're told to.

What has this got to do with going beyond audacity? I believe we are all divinely built to create and grow, and that this will never change. We've heard the phrase **BHAG** (**B**ig, **H**airy, **A**udacious **G**oals) that have been popularly thrown at us. I'm still a big believer in striving and stretching – but I'm not letting myself be obsessed by them, or allow them to taunt me if I don't achieve all of them. Sometimes, it's also a case of not the right time.

At this point of penning this down, something is not aligned with the spirit; for example, you don't feel aligned with your work anymore. Now, before you quit your job because you're not happy, **write down exactly what is not**

making you happy. You can blame people, the environment, or politics for that matter – but really, get down to the core of it.

If it's your boss, what can you do about it? Will it warrant a conversation? If you're tired (and grouchy) all the time, could it actually be the time spent travelling to and from work? There are many reasons. Sometimes, it could just be a misalignment of values. **Be clear as to why you're not happy – and get deep.**

I went to see the Malaysian Philharmonic Orchestra a few years ago. If you've been there before, this is what happens: people are moving and talking; the musicians are tuning their instruments, creating an actual cacophony of sounds. Suddenly, the conductor comes in. Everyone is seated; mobile phones are put away; and complete silence fills the room. The conductor raises his baton, and magic happens harmonically and melodically.

You are the conductor of your life. When you remove the noise, you will know the direction you are heading in. It's a bit like social media where we are busy liking, following, and friending other people: Are you liking, following, and friending yourself? We all know the right steps in our heart of hearts.

I am actually the sort of person who would consult people I respect and trust to get their feedback on a particular situation. I do take notes when I am in a meeting, and I write down different perspectives so that I am not blindsided – but at the end of the day, after looking at it from various angles, I have to make a decision on what my next step is. On a spiritual level, I do pray about things, and ask for wisdom and discernment about the right direction I need to take.

A Reason, A Season, or A Lifetime

Who do you surround yourself with? Do you have friends or acquaintances in the various directions of your life, based on the Wheel of Life that we talked about in the previous chapter? Initially, I made friendships unconsciously, regardless of which direction they fit – but now, I prefer to make conscious decisions.

To get better and different perspectives of life, I find that these friendships have helped me to be more well-rounded. Interestingly, if you don't have friends in a particular area, it means that's one thing you're not working on. For example, if you don't have friends or associates in the area of fitness, you're probably not doing any exercise at all! True or false?

These friends can be there for a reason; they can be there for a season; or they can be there for a lifetime. Whatever the case may be, conversations with these will veer in certain directions accordingly. To see what I mean, let's get back to my friends in fitness. More than 10 years ago, I deliberately wanted to make fitness a priority and an integral part of my lifestyle – so I joined a bootcamp. And guess what? I would meet those who have continued to be my friends for walks, runs, or hikes – or just for exercising together. Remember, birds of a feather flock together.

Unconsciously, they keep me on my toes in fitness – and the same goes for the other areas of my life. As such, it's necessary for you to look at your Wheel of Life and identify what sort of friends or acquaintances are missing; it's usually an indication of what's missing in your life that prevents you from living a truly audacious and fulfilled life.

Sustaining the Audacity

What does sustainability have to do with an audacious life? (No, it's not just about climate change – but that's also important, and everything is interlinked anyway.) Recently, the 17 Sustainable Development Goals (SDGs) piqued my interest. They seem like something so grandly gigantic that only large corporations or governments should be taking the lead on them rather than us mere individuals.

It got me thinking about what sustainability means to me, and what I can do as an individual using tools in design thinking. It's not only about me having the means to be sustainable – money helps, of course – but also what I can do to **help** sustainability.

One thing that matters to me is gender equality – so I thought about what I could do to help that cause. I broke it down further in terms of what I am immediately connected to: business. Globally, only 30% of businesses are owned by women – and only about 20% here in Malaysia.

How will things change if 50% of businesses are owned by women – and what can I do to change the equation? In the capacity of what I do, I always support women-owned businesses by buying from them first, and also sharing their stories in my role as a journalist. So, yes: **dig deep**. What area of sustainability resonates with you – and if you break it down to bite-sized pieces, what can you, as an individual, do?

The Queen Elsa Recommendation

A business mentor and friend of mine said that for people to achieve more, they should hang around people who are doing better than them. And as much as we are enamoured with billionaires like Elon Musk and Sir Richard Branson, perhaps we can start a little smaller. For example, if you earn a million in revenue, perhaps you should meet people who earn 10. If you earn 10, hang around the people who earn 50, so that you get a bigger perspective – but are not overwhelmed at the same time.

I apply that method personally – and most times, it need not be extrinsic or intrinsic. I will admit that I am going through some life-changing decisions at the moment. A decade ago, I would be caught in a whirlwind. Nowadays, I may be still be in a whirlwind – but I can recognise it, can step away from it, and I will know the steps I need to take.

Over the years, I gained more tools in my arsenal to recognise the thought processes that I need to go through. Sometimes, it's a case of asking myself if I am better today than I was yesterday – and it can be from many aspects of life. I look back at how far I have come – and I appreciate that I need not compare myself with anyone.

If something doesn't pan out, breathe, and learn to let it go. Even if it means fighting your motherly instincts when your man-child leaves the nest.

Your Permanently Audacious Life

by Bavani Periasamy

The world can be a challenging place. In order to get the most out of life, we often need to step outside of our comfort zone to do things that we never dreamt we were capable of doing. We should never shy away from life and live timidly. We need to challenge ourselves, and always grow beyond our perceived limitations.

In other words, we need to live audaciously.

When all is said and done, "audacity" is not just a word. It should not be limited to instances of courage by individuals who found it within themselves to step out. Audacity should be much more than that. Audacity is a way of life. It's the willingness and the courage to live one's truth and to pursue one's dreams.

The world needs audacious people who are willing to take risks, take responsibility, and have the courage to be themselves.

We need audacious people who can inspire others with their actions and words. We need audacious people who will stand up for what they believe in – even if it means standing alone. We need audacious people who will never give up on their dreams, no matter what others say or do.

The world is full of people who are living audaciously – and they are the ones who lead by example. They are the ones who inspire us to live our best lives, and to never settle for anything less than what we deserve.

Audacity isn't just about being brave in the face of fear; it's about fighting against injustice, dreaming without limits, and daring to be different. It's about living an extraordinary life that makes a difference in the world.

When I think about going beyond audacity, what comes to mind is that it's actually a part of us, in the way we live our lives. So, in order to move beyond audacity, we have to embrace audacity – and make it the norm instead of the exception. We have to be brave and comfortable enough to always practice the traits that is typically used to define audacious behaviour. Here are four ways to incorporate audacity into your genetic makeup:

1. Speak up

Regardless of our racial heritage, us Malaysians are often taught from a young age not to go against the grain. The need to follow the consensus and not go against it is entrenched in the *rakyat*. In fact, there is a Malay proverb that says: "*Bulat air kerana pembentung, Bulat manusia kerana muafakat.*" – which carries the meaning that "Consensus is imperative for unity." As a result of this, Malaysians seldom want to speak up.

This, however, should not be the case. In one of my early jobs, the HR head at the time often urged us to always challenge everything. He believed that ideas need to be challenged in order to improve and strengthen them. In his words: "Diamonds are formed only after intense pressure."

As such, we should not be afraid to speak up. In fact, we should make our voices heard.

It may seem better for some people to just be keepers: keep quiet, keep your thoughts to yourself, and keep the peace. However, it may be that we actually have something priceless to contribute to the discussion. Our point of view may have great value – it would be selfish for us to not share. Even if it turns out that we were not accurate in what we wanted to say, at least we made an effort to put forward our thoughts to the discussion at hand. We need to have confidence in ourselves to voice our thoughts out.

But, being confident and speaking up is not always easy. In order to find your voice, you need to find what you care about and what you want for yourself. Once you know this, it will be much easier for you to speak up. You will have something worth fighting for – and that will give you the courage to stand up for yourself and for those around you. We need to be bold enough to speak their minds without fear of being ridiculed. That is the audacity that we need to make part of our daily lives

2. Take risks

Many of us are very hesitant when it comes to taking risks. We often tell ourselves that it would be better to play it safe, in fear that we would compromise our current positions. What we sometimes fail to recognise is that we seldom get to improve ourselves or our situation without taking risks.

In a way, playing it safe is a huge risk by itself in the long run.

Before taking risks, though, it is important to first do a risk-reward analysis. This would greatly help in easing our fears when we move towards a new direction. I have always looked at risks from a few angles. Some risks have a good chance of succeeding – but there is also the potential for failure. And some risks encapsulate both these outcomes. These are the risks that we should usually take on, as the chances for success is there with lower chances for failure.

Some risks have a low chance of success but also have the potential for great rewards. These are sometimes called Hail Mary situations (to borrow from American football jargon). It is sometimes tempting for some to go for these risks, in view of the reward – but it is best to think it through before going ahead with these.

Lastly, there are risks where everything can go wrong – and can fail in a big way. I think that I should not have to say that we should avoid these risks as much as we possibly can.

An audacious person is usually more willing to take on risks in order to improve their lot in life. I feel that in order to move beyond audacity, we should be more open to accepting risks and be more intelligent in deciding which risks are worthy to undertake.

3. Live up to your values/principles

As I wrote these chapters, the one key thing that I had been constantly reflecting upon was that in everything I do, in all the decisions I made and in all the times when I was audacious, I had been mindful to always remember the values that are most important to me. These values are something I hold close to my heart – and knowing that these values are important to me helps me make decisions when it comes to speaking up and taking risks. Being audacious comes with responsibilities – and for me, one of them is to stay true to my values and principles.

This is especially important because our values and principles form the core of who we are; they define us. By ensuring that we stick to these values and principles, we know that we are staying true to ourselves – even in our moments of audacity.

You may notice that some of these are intertwined with one another. Why do I say that? Because in speaking up, it's also about speaking up about what is right for you, and standing up for it. Living up to our values sometimes requires us to make decisions based on the here and now when its right for you – it may be the biggest decision you will ever have to make.

4. Believe

Belief is one important element in my life. I think I will not be where I am today if I did not have belief. Yes, there were many instances I had doubts and worries, including the concerns that people around me also helped me have. But as I look back now, I know there was this belief that an Indian girl like me from a small town called Port Dickson could also do big things. With belief, I knew that if I could hold it up in my mind, it would only be a matter of time before it becomes true.

With belief, there is also a sense of hope and faith that comes with it; it is these that make things possible. A favourite quote of mine is from Napoleon Hill:

> *"Whatever the mind can conceive and believe,*
> *the mind can achieve regardless of*
> *how many times you may have failed in the past or*
> *how lofty your aims and hopes may be."*

He wrote this in his 1937 book *Think and Grow Rich* – and again, as I reflect, there have been many instances where my dreams were audacious (big and close to unbelievable), but it was a matter of time before they came to reality.

As I draw a close to my contributions for this book, this is what I would like to share: The key is that it may not seem like it's audacious anymore after a while because it has become a way of being. You may not think that what you are doing is big and bold – because it has become the way you live, and it has now become congruent within your body, mind, and spirit. You know you are doing what's right for you and the community you live in; and you know you are championing for what is right and – most importantly – for what that matters to you.

We women all have the audacity in us to go for what we want; to stand up and to speak up for what's right, and to make the decisions which otherwise we may not make or take – because we are worthy, and because we are more than enough. What we want to have, what we wish to have, our success – all belong to us; it becomes ours, when we are audacious.

Step Up and Step Beyond

by Fu-En Yee

You have already read what audacity is all about. Coming from six different perspectives (including mine), you now know in general that audacity simply can be concluded as: **bravely being your authentic self**.

In addition, you were also exposed to a diverse group of authors with various experiences: from the corporate world, to professionals, all the way to entrepreneurial scenes – and also the perspectives of those who are/were single, married, or divorced. What you read also covered the art and science of how to be audacious.

We shared real stories of how we stuck strongly to our values to create the results we have today, despite going through hell and all sorts of nightmares – after all, being audacious also means being courageous to pursue what we feel is right. With our combined experiences over a cumulative period of more than 300 years – yikes – it is our express hope that you can relate to some of our personal stories and case studies, and to find the needed strength to rise up for yourself.

What we have shared throughout this book is a series of gifts and benefits that being audacious gets you, to motivate you to stand up and step up and create the life you truly want. We want you to tap into both your head and heart, and listen to that inner voice that is screaming desperately for your attention. It wants you to be free from beliefs, traditions, cultures, and expectations that are no longer supportive of where you yearn to go.

Increase Your Awareness

In this final chapter, it is our invitation for you to start taking the necessary steps to be who you truly are and what you really want to achieve in life. Clearly, that means you need to do some self-discovery, self-searching on who you are:

- What are your true values?
- What are your real needs?
- What is the life purpose that you want to live for?
- What is it that you simply cannot tolerate?
- What do you stand for?

Among all these steps, the foundational work is the hardest and toughest, as it requires awareness. As human beings are all creatures of habits, everything seems to already be on autopilot. Awareness cannot happen in that state. There will be times when you say: "Enough is enough!" – and you have to seriously mean it. That is where and when you start your journey. You need to pause and reflect, then ask yourself "Why?":

- Why am I feeling this?

- Why am I unhappy; stressed; anxious; frustrated; angry?

- Why am I struggling with…?

- Why do I always get triggered by certain words, people, behaviours, or environment?

Discovering the cycles of pain, paying attention to their frequency; catching yourself falling into the habits of numbing distractions (all kinds of gratification); and sometimes playing the "victim game" – these can all be extremely uncomfortable. You will need to take note of the frequency of such cycles, and noticing the triggers.

When I say "Take note", I mean journaling it down – not take note "in the brain". The brain has limitless space for storage – and that is the problem: since it has limitless space, it cannot sense the "urgency", or how critical it is. It will not alert you on how many times you had gone through that cycle.

It is entirely different when you jot it down in a diary or a booklet: it becomes obvious, because you can count. I have heard from my clients' own admission again and again what a huge difference it made between journaling it physically and noting it just in the brain.

The more you are aware, the more that you can note – the faster you get to see how critical it is, and the faster you will want to get to the root of things to understand the whole of you. When you peel the onion layer by layer, you get tears in your eyes – painful, uncomfortable, and very disturbing – but you will get to the juiciest part of the core.

Actions – Progression, Not Perfection

Keep in mind that no one is perfect. There is no definite measurement for audacity. Each of us has our own understanding of what being audacious is about – and all six of us came from different perspectives of how to be audacious.

You may have your own version of what audacity mean to you – at varied levels too.

As long as you are progressing towards being your true self – unashamed, and serving from your heart – then that is good enough. **It is not a race; rather, it is a journey to become your true self.** Understand that you want to do this because each and every individual on Earth has own unique purpose – and it is your birth right to be who you are truly meant to be.

Relax and chill. Never compare your progress with another person's. **All progression is good, regardless of speed.** This is your personal excursion of self-actualisation – and the earlier you commence this excursion, the more you will be able to find out if you detoured into a wrong direction, and the faster you can take corrective measures; and ultimately, the earlier you can then reach your chosen destination.

Did you know that the Apollo moon rockets were off course 97% of the time?

If you pose the same question to all your friends, I can assure you that only the few very well-read ones would admit knowing this. Just like the rockets, we constantly need to be aware when we go off track, then quickly take the necessary actions to get back on the right one. After all, 97% of the time means **almost all of the time**.

Every time you catch yourself falling back into your comfort zone of the autopilot, remind yourself of the reason why you want to get out from that cycle. It is imperative – because then you will be able to keep yourself on track for what you are supposed to be working on.

Accountability – A Journey Together

I believe that this is the key to unlocking the fullest potential of where you could go. It is very common for you to start doubting and questioning if being audacious seriously works for you – especially when your own family and friends make remarks about how much you have changed.

Welcome to the real world. This is where you are no longer accommodating to what you used to be, and you are no longer the "same" as you used to be. Facing naysayers; criticism; having people who (in)directly weigh you down; who slow you and stop you from progressing – these are just some extra weights that can push you upto help you to go further.

What you need is an environment that continues to motivate, encourage, and lift you to reach where you want to go: what you need are **"accountability" friends**. These are friends who care about your growth and happiness, who want to help to free yourself, who are in the same journey, and who want to achieve the same as you.

In Chinese, we have a proverb: "You can easily break one chopstick – but when bundled together, it becomes unbreakable and incredibly strong." This reflects unity – and represents why when you have such friends standing by your side cheering you on, then there is nothing you cannot achieve. **By sticking together for the same purpose, we become an indestructible whole**.

In my first book, *Boss, Your Wish Is Your Command!*, I suggested SPICE as a means of creating an environment that supports growth. It stands for the following:

Support	Play the supportive role when you hit challenges
Promote	As the 3rd eye to look out on what else can be done
Induce	Consistently realign and keep you on track
Commit	Cheerlead to keep you committed to your growth
Encourage	The motivator who provides constructive feedback

You may be thinking: it will be a challenge to have five friends to work alongside with you on this. You don't have to. Your friends or colleagues can play more than one role: for example, a friend can take up three roles of Support (S), Commit (C) and Encourage (E), while another friend does Promote (P) and Induce (I).

I believe having two friends is very much more doable.

Among the five roles above, C is the most vital for most Asians. We have a shared culture that has shaped us to be very humble – overly humble, in fact. We are also extra critical to ourselves; we belittle your achievements, and even more sadly, we rarely celebrate our own successes.

Why? Because they mostly seem to be "pretty average achievements"; "It was expected"; or the most frequent statement of "You're just lucky". As such, the friend who is supposed to carry the C role must be able to notice all the achievements, growths, and improvements that have taken place – no matter how small that is.

Make sure your friends know the reason(s) why you want to be audacious – and they will want to support your journey. Be clear about their roles – and be specific about how they can be of your support.

I mentioned in Chapter 2 that one may "want" to be audacious, but may "not be necessarily ready" nor "willing" to be audacious. Not many will be ready nor willing. **This process is easy; it is, however, crucial – and it will be most liberating once you got through this.**

I invite you to take on this journey. If my audacious sisters and I can do this, I am super confident that you can too.

No one is born to be a victim. Unfortunately, over the years, you had unknowingly surrendered your power to other people. Instead of making decisions based on what your heart wants, you allowed others to decide for you. You yearned for love, attention, and care from those around you – so, you sacrificed your own to fulfil other people's needs.

And all that ever gained you was heartache, disappointments, and frustrations of why other people did not appreciate or reciprocate with the same manner.

If you want to set yourself free and be who you truly are, audacity is the way forward. Only you can be the one to create the life you want. Everything begins with your intention to be one.

Step out. Step up.

It is time to think for yourself. Take actions to be yourself.

We look forward having more of you to embark on this journey.

Contact the Authors

If you would like to get in touch with the authors for keynote and work engagement, you can reach them here at

info@InspiredLifeInternational.com

Drop Us a Book Review

If you like what you read and would like to share a book review to encourage the authors, you can visit the book page here.

www.theinspirationhub.com/dare